to Catherine
with
love and light,
    anna Ogvesly

My New Friend, Grief

Reflections on Loss and Life

Anna Hodges Oginsky

BALBOA.
PRESS

A DIVISION OF HAY HOUSE

Balboa Press books may be ordered through booksellers or by contacting:

Balboa Press
A Division of Hay House
1663 Liberty Drive
Bloomington, IN 47403
www.balboapress.com
1 (877) 407-4847

Print information available on the last page.

ISBN: 978-1-5043-5650-3 (sc)
ISBN: 978-1-5043-5651-0 (e)

Library of Congress Control Number: 2016906574

Balboa Press rev. date: 06/16/2016

James Shields Hodges III, wrote the original lyrics for the song "Nothin' But Love" as they are printed here in this book. It is with deep gratitude for his art that the author shares them with you.

For Daniel, James, Alexander, and Sophia
Thank you for choosing me.

Contents

Dear Sweet Reader

If you are reading this book because you have experienced the loss of someone you love, please accept my deepest condolences. I know that your grief is as unique to you as your fingerprint. You are likely to be experiencing a broad range of emotions. Please know that all of these emotions are okay to be feeling—even if they don't always make sense. My wish for you is that you find some comfort and maybe even some hope in these pages. I would consider it a privilege to be your companion as you grieve your own loss. Thank you for giving me the opportunity to sit with you.

If you are reading this book because you have experienced some other kind of loss or for any other reason, thank you. The same goes for you. We are in this together, and I am honored to be here by your side. Possibly one of the most unexpected outcomes of witnessing another person's grief is the ways in which it can provoke or trigger your own grief—perhaps buried deep inside. You may not have even have known you carried that grief with you. If unexpected feelings arise while reading my story, know that this is normal. Whatever comes up for you is okay. Maybe it has been waiting for an opportunity to rise.

After someone dies, we flood those who remain—those who cherished the deceased most dearly—with love. We rush to support them in any way we can. We bring nourishing meals for the grieving, we send cards to let them know they are not alone, we share our memories of their loved ones to express how their lives mattered to us, and we absorb their salty tears on our shoulders. As a recipient of this outpouring of support and kindness when my dad unexpectedly passed away in 2010, I am eternally grateful. I felt loved and connected to those I loved in ways I had never experienced. I was surprised to learn that people cared enough about me to share my loss with me. I was also surprised to learn that people who I thought cared a great deal about me didn't seem to see my pain at all. As the date on the calendar moved further from the day of my dad's funeral, my feeling of being buoyed by that love and support faded. The afternoons where my dad had once shown up at my house to help me with my children and take my leftovers home for his lunch the next day were completely void of what I had come to rely on. All around me, people were going on with their lives as if nothing earth-shattering had happened.

I became intimate with loneliness. It seemed as if everything that had happened, from the horrific night my dad died to the moments I spent waving good-bye to the hearse after his funeral, had merely been a very bad dream. I was exhausted. I felt empty and alone. I wondered why we don't create more space for grief and the grieving in our society. I wondered why we don't talk more about loss. I wondered why people looked away when I wanted to talk about my loss.

Death plays an essential role in the unfolding of our life stories. Instead of embracing death as a part of the process of life, we typically fear it. When we face death or the loss of a loved one, we often hide behind obligatory smiles and say, "I am fine." We may look fine on the outside while we feel lost, afraid, hopeless, and alone. We say we are fine, but we are far from it. I didn't think I had a choice except to say that I was doing fine when someone asked me how I was doing.

"And how is your mom?" "She is fine."

"And your sister?" "Sarah is fine too. We're all fine."

I felt pressured to move on, to heal, and to get over it. I knew I was expected to be strong for my mom and be happy for everyone else because "that's what your dad would have wanted." If I only knew one thing about my dad, it was that what he aspired to in life was to be real—to remain true to himself. Despite what people told me, I knew that what he would have wanted was for me to be real too. To be real, and to honor my dad, I would need to face the fact that I wouldn't always feel fine, or be happy or strong.

Shortly after my dad died, in the midst of sorrow, confusion, and wondering how it could have played out differently—under different circumstances—my mom read a book that suggested we acknowledge a person's death in the same way we do his or her birth. It suggested that we not question this leg of the journey—not doubt it or dread it—and honor it instead. At first, I couldn't imagine that as a possibility. I keep returning to that invitation though, and I have come to sincerely appreciate it. If we were to truly honor and even celebrate death, to revere it with the same awe and wonder we do birth—not just as part of the life cycle or process but as a milestone in a person's life—maybe it wouldn't be so hard to live with loss. If instead of fearing it and fighting it, we embraced it as a person's last meaningful act on earth, we might feel less alone in our grief. Maybe more of us would share our stories about the ways we experience loss.

I share my story here imagining that you may recognize your own grief in these glimpses of mine. I hope this will serve as a reminder that you are not alone. Losing my dad certainly broadened my understanding of death and loss, but more importantly, experiencing this loss expanded my understanding of life and what it means to live. It taught me that there is always another way—another way of being, of living, and of doing. Where I once was closed off to the world around and within me, I have opened. Where I was too hard, I softened. Where I once gave way to fear, I made space for love. Where I once felt powerless, I am now empowered. Where I once saw a lack of love and resources to sustain me, I now see an abundance of love and resources for every person on this planet.

One of my all-time favorite quotes comes from Anaïs Nin. She said, "And the day came when the risk to remain tight in a bud was more painful than the risk it took to blossom." We begin as tiny little seeds filled with potential. As we grow into our lives, we harden. We tighten into tiny little buds. If we are lucky, we realize how tightly wound we are, and we recognize that we cannot bear to spend another day in that kind of bind. It can be scary to let go of our defenses and break free from that tiny bud. It can be really scary, especially when everything we have ever known put us in that bud. We feel safe there. We know how to operate from that bud. We may take a few steps forward and a few steps back before we are fully ready to bloom. We may read a lot of books and blogs about the ways other people have bloomed. We may be inspired. We may be overwhelmed.

The process of blooming, or really the process of life, is not an easy one to navigate by any stretch of the imagination. No prayer or platitude can eliminate the harsh pain of the things that hurt us. But when we finally take the risk to really, truly bloom into a new way of being or thinking or acting in our lives, it is liberating. I was liberated by my grief.

Looking back at my life story, I can see how the challenges that bent and broke me when I faced them also blessed and strengthened me in ways I could not have imagined when they occurred. Taking the risk to blossom is all about living in possibility. It is about choosing another way to live, to be, and to show up in the world. Blossoming means facing our fears, doubts, and shame instead of hiding from them. It means naming those things that are buried deep inside you—calling them out from the darkness and into the light—and taking back the power they held over you.

This is a book about how my life experiences shaped my beliefs about death and loss and how my perception shifted when I realized that befriending grief would allow me to move through life in richer and more meaningful ways.

Wherever you are, I wish you peace on your journey.

He's in the Shed

We turned down their road. It was the only road I had ever known as theirs. They lived in the same house for thirty-seven years. It was out in the boondocks, as we used to say—the boonies. Way out in the country, on a dirt road.

After Dan and I visited my parents there, at their house for the first time, Dan told me that he had been nervous as he drove—farther and farther—wondering where I could possibly be taking him. After miles of winding, hilly, and narrow dirt roads, Webberdale Road seems to appear out of nowhere. By that night, about seventeen years later, Dan could have driven those roads with his eyes closed. He knew where to let up on the gas pedal because the hills were steep, where to look out for cars coming from the opposite direction because the road was about to narrow to almost one lane, and where the road twisted around so sharply, we could very easily land in a swamp if he wasn't careful.

It was raining that night and probably had been for days. Potholes that threatened to swallow us whole covered Webberdale. Every few bumps, I felt my stomach lurch up into my throat. I remembered Dan driving those roads when

I was pregnant, worried that taking the bumps too hard would force me into labor. I turned around in my seat to look at our three sleeping children in the back of the car.

Dan had given me three options after he told me that my mom had called while I was out running an errand that night. After he told me that my mom found my dad in the shed. After he told me that she thought he was dead. She was a nurse. If my dad was dead when she found him, I knew she would know it. My options were 1) Dan could leave and go to my parents' house. 2) I could leave and go to my parents' house. 3) We could stay together.

We would wake up the kids and take them to my parents' house with us. I hated the thought of waking the kids, and ordinarily, I wouldn't have chosen to do that, but this situation was far from ordinary. I was scared. I needed Dan. I couldn't imagine hearing the worst news I had ever heard without him by my side. I also needed my kids with me. I couldn't imagine facing the loss of my dad without the reminder that my children provided—that I had to be okay because I am a mom, and a mom's job is to be okay.

My parents' house is about halfway down Webberdale. As we approached, I saw an ambulance parked in the road in front of their house. The lights were flashing, and the back doors were flung wide open, but there wasn't anyone around. The driveway was lined with my mom's black Subaru, my dad's gray Ford pickup truck, and a police car.

I decided to go check things out while Dan waited in the car with our sleeping beauties. As soon as I stepped out of the car, I sank into the mud. Crowded by overgrown bushes, my parents' driveway could barely fit the width of a car, and I struggled to walk around the cars that were there. I kept my head down, trying to keep the rain from falling into my eyes. I heard a man's voice in the dark.

"Are you the daughter?" he asked.

I looked up, searching for his face, and tried to register his question. "Uh, yeah. Yeah, I'm the daughter."

"Your mom is in the house, and the MSP is in the back with your dad."

The MSP is in the back with my dad? "Oh. So, is he okay then?" I pictured my dad in the shed telling jokes to the MSP, whoever that was.

"Um, I hate to be the one to tell you this, ma'am, but your dad slipped away." The man's voice trailed off, also slipping away. His words hit me like a hard punch in the gut. The blow sped up my trunk, blasting a hole in my heart. A lump formed in my throat.

"Oh," I think I said. Even years later, I can still see the sympathetic expression on his face. I imagine he felt sorry for me, yet he didn't know me. He didn't know my dad, but he was the one who told me—even though he hated to—that my dad had slipped away. I looked down at the car next to me. I was using it to keep my balance. It said Michigan State Police across the side. "Oh." I was catching on. "And the MSP is the Michigan State Police?"

"Right," he said. His voice was soft when he asked, "Do you need help?"

Nothing seemed certain from that point forward, but one thing I knew was that I did not need help. I did not want help. The man who told me that my dad slipped away headed out to the road, and I made my way to the house. I opened the front door and yelled for my mom. The smell of my parents' house overwhelmed me. It still smelled a little like woodstove to me, even though many years had passed since my dad took the woodstove out of the house. And it smelled like my dad's earthy, musky scent. His smell hung in the house like the smell of burning leaves hangs in the air in autumn. The house was dark, except for a dim light glowing in the kitchen. The entryway was cluttered with my dad's boots and my parents' slippers. A hat rack stood next to the doorway with a hat from my dad's collection on each branch. There was a beret. A Stormy Kromer. A baseball cap. There were books, catalogs, and magazines piled on end tables and on the floor. I sighed, wondering how my parents found their way through the clutter. I wished, like I had so many times as a little girl in that very same house, for a clear path out of there. I searched the whole house, yelling, "Mom?"

My mom didn't answer.

I opened the sliding glass door in the back of the house and saw flashlights and what looked like people crowded in the door of my dad's shed. Woody's World. He had carved the sign out of wood and hung it on the door to his shed. Woody was one of my dad's nicknames. Big Red was another. His grandchildren called him Papaw. The shed was Woody's World. Almost anytime I called the house to talk to my mom and asked what my dad was doing, she would say, "He's in the shed."

I yelled out the door, "Mom?"

"Anna! Oh Anna," my mom wailed in an unrecognizable voice. In eighteen years of living with her and in thirty-seven years of knowing her, I had never heard her wail like that.

I tried to make my way to the shed as quickly as possible, but I kept hitting patches of ice, slipping, and sinking into the mud surrounding the ice. It was early March in Michigan, and we were dancing between the deep freeze of winter and the promise of a thaw in spring. The ice was starting to melt due to the recent rain, but in the dark, I couldn't tell the difference between ice and mud and solid ground.

It was still raining, my mom was wailing, I was slipping, and flashlights were shining in my face. It felt more like a scene from a psychological thriller than it did my own life in my parents' backyard. The men surrounding my mom formed a line to help me to the shed. It seemed like there were hundreds of men, but there were only about four. One by one, they grabbed my elbow and guided me forward.

The last man in the row stood in the doorway of the shed. He had been shining his flashlight down to light my path, and he stepped back so I could step into the shed. There was barely enough room for me to stand. My mom was nestled next to a police officer who looked just like my cousin Greg, and my dad sat peacefully at his workbench.

My dad was hunched over with his eyes closed, and he looked like he always did when he fell asleep on my couch, waiting for my mom to gather her stuff so they could leave. The book he was reading stood on its end on the floor next to him, looking like it had dropped right out of his hand. His long, soft, shiny white hair was pulled back into a ponytail, and other than a few extra layers of clothing he must have added when he got home, he looked no different than he did hours earlier when he left my house. He didn't look dead to me. But I will admit that he did look as if he had slipped away. His face held no expression—nothing that indicated his presence. He looked like he had slipped right out of his body like a snail does when it leaves its shell. The shell becomes but a souvenir, a remnant of the life lived inside it. I wanted to scoop up his body and hold it just like I would a shell on the beach, but I could only stare. I watched him for only a few moments. I had to look away. I turned my attention toward my sobbing mother.

By that time, Officer Greg had gently suggested that I take my mom inside the house. Again, nothing seemed sure then, and I really had no idea what would be the right thing to do, but I knew that nobody could make my mom go into the house if she didn't want to go into the house. Officer Greg didn't know what he was up against. Just to be nice, and possibly to avoid being arrested for disobeying a police officer, I asked my mom to go inside with me. She said no. I wasn't surprised.

I looked around the shed. My dad had hung parts of his collection of antique saws from the ceiling. He had posted a few notes on the walls, and I spotted one that said something about the edge of darkness. I felt like I had fallen over the edge of darkness. The collective impact of the dark sky, the saws hanging from the ceiling, the notes my dad left behind, and his dead body there before me was huge. I could feel myself beginning to unravel. I tried to keep it all together.

I was shocked—but not shocked enough to burst into tears in front of a bunch of strange men. I suspected that the tide had forever changed the landscape of my life. On some level, I knew that it was now my job to remain strong for my mom and my kids. Even though I stood there—as a grown woman, a wife, and a mother of three little ones—a small, childlike voice inside me wondered what these men thought of my dad and his shed. I wondered if they found the saws hanging from the ceiling as creepy as I did. I wondered if the scene looked suspicious to their discerning eyes.

"Mom, you can stay as long as you need to, but I can't stay here with you. Dan and the kids are in the car. I need to tell them what's going on," I said. I looked at her, trying to read her, and she looked at me and nodded. She wanted me to do what I needed to do. One of the men gave me his flashlight, and I slowly made my way back to the road and my waiting family.

I was relieved to see that all three of our children were still asleep when I got back to the car. I never imagined having to tell my husband that my dad was dead. When I did, Dan got out the car and held me as I sobbed into his shoulder. The rain fell around us and all over us. I was soaked with tears and rain and disbelief. Dan took our children home, and I walked back into my parents' house.

It wasn't long before my mom joined me in the house. She didn't want to leave my dad even though Officer Greg had assured her that he would stay with my dad until the coroner arrived and that he would keep my dad safe. While I believe in my heart that Officer Greg and his cohorts would gladly give my mom a free pass to stay as long as she needed to, I also knew they had work to do. And it was cold and rainy and dark where that work was to be done. There were saws hanging over their heads and words taped to the walls. They needed my mom out of the shed to do that work, and as frightening as that seemed to me, I understood.

Later, my mom shared that she had asked Officer Greg if he would make his own mother leave his father in a situation like that. He said his mother had no choice but to leave his dad when he passed away because she had small children to care for. Greg was one of those small children. I pictured a young woman, a mother, finding her husband dead in their home with no choice but to leave his side. I pictured her returning to her children. How did she face them? What did she say? How did she possibly go on? And yet, here Officer Greg stood, living proof that even after the most unimaginable tragedies, people live on.

I was being initiated into a new society, reaching a new milestone in my life. I joined the sad ranks of children who had lost a parent. A new level of understanding of life and death and how we deal with it opened up for me that night. The image of Greg's mother leaving her dead husband's side to care for her small children haunts me. It wasn't long before we counted the fact that my mom's own children were grown when she lost her husband among the many blessings for which we were grateful.

Before my mom came into the house, she prayed with my dad. This quiet moment with him allowed her to make peace with needing to leave his side. I recently listened in as she told my oldest son, James, what happened the night his Papaw died. My mom told James she thought my dad was sleeping. She said, "Shields? Did you fall asleep?" She began CPR as soon as she realized that he was not sleeping. She made her way back into the house to call 911, my sister, and me, and then she went back to his side.

I can hardly allow myself to imagine what that must have been like for her. Waiting, in the house, for her husband to come in to share the dinner he left on the stove while he went out to his shed to read or finish up a few things. She would have been waiting, getting settled back at home after a long day out and about, and then eventually wondering when he would come in for dinner. He would have known that she was home by then. She would decide to go check on him despite their understanding that the shed was his domain. She would worry about intruding as she made her way out to the shed in the rain, through the mud and the melting ice, thinking he might be sleeping. And finally, she would open the door to the shed, peering around the corner and seeing him there—calling out his name. She would check his pulse. Find there was none. Try to bring him back, all the while knowing he was gone, and wanting it not to be true. After all that, the time she spent in prayer with him was essential to beginning the long, impossible process of trying to let him go.

When she came inside, I was sitting on a beautiful old green fainting couch that my parents had inherited from my Baba, my dad's mother. It was my favorite napping spot when I visited Baba as a little girl, and it really was my favorite piece of furniture at her house. The fainting couch and I had been through a lot together. We conspired in acting out very dramatic fake fainting spells right into my teenage years. The beautiful green couch was there—first at Baba's house and then at my parents'—to comfort me when I needed to be comforted. When I was too old to run to the arms of my grandmother or my parents for comfort, I went to her: the fainting couch. The green slope cradled me like a huge arm. It felt right to return to her then and to let that old, green lady hold me in her arm again.

My mom sat down next to me. We turned our heads to face each other, neither of us quite sure what to do. I can still picture my mom's expression in that moment. A dullish gray tone had taken over her sparkly blue eyes. She looked frightened and tired and old. She had never looked old to me. She said, "Anna, you girls think I'm so strong, but I'm not. I got all my strength from your dad."

I wanted to shake her and scream, "You liar!"

My mom is a very private person, but what I know of her life was that it wasn't always easy. It was rarely easy. Despite the challenges she faced, at every stage of her life, she persevered. She kept going, living fully and with an open heart when she could risk keeping it open. I am quite confident that she is by far the strongest woman I have ever known. I didn't believe her, but I was afraid of what might happen if she was right. I was afraid of the possibility that somehow I had missed her bluff and that, for all these years, she really was getting all her strength from my dad. I think she needed me to know that she could not be strong in that moment, that she wasn't feeling strong at all, and that she didn't foresee feeling strong anytime soon. She had been strong for so long. Maybe she was giving up on strong.

Another officer came inside and asked us if we needed anything. He surprised us with his question. We looked at each other and back at him. My mom and I didn't know what we needed.

"What do people normally need in this situation?" I asked.

"Well, some people request a priest. Something like that," he said.

My mom and I again looked at each other, dumbfounded. We didn't want a priest. My dad wouldn't have wanted a priest.

I thought of something. "We haven't been able to reach my sister," I said.

He seemed relieved to be able to help us and told us that he would send a state trooper to her home in Ann Arbor. I pictured Sarah riding to my parents' house in the back of a police car. I was so desperate to reach her that I didn't mind subjecting her to a ride in the back of a police car. She and her husband Nate didn't have a landline at their house. As her older, less tech-savvy sister, I thought that was really irresponsible. A ride in a police car seemed fitting for her.

When Sarah did finally call us that night, she said she wanted to see my dad before the coroner took him away, but we were running out of time. I looked over my mom's shoulder, toward the shed where my dad's body and all that surrounded it was being examined. Flashes from the coroner's camera lit the dark, rainy night.

It occurred to me that we didn't know what caused my dad to die. It was an unexpected realization. Of course, nothing that happened that night could have been expected, and anytime I stopped to consider the circumstances of the night, my only conclusion was that it was all so unusual. The one thing that did make sense to me was that my dad died in his shed. It made perfect sense to me. He built that crazy shed with plywood and 2x4s and his own two hands. His shed and his Ford pickup truck were the two places where he spent most of his time. As ominous as the shed seemed to me that night, I knew it was my dad's escape from the outside world and that he loved it. The shed was a clubhouse for one in a forest of trees. It seemed so appropriate that my dad slipped away from inside his shed. I don't think he would have had it any other way.

In her conversation with James, my mom said she wished she had been with my dad when he died.

James said, "Maybe Papaw got a message that he was supposed to die alone."

Message received.

As the coroner's camera flashed, I wondered briefly whether my mom was a suspect in my dad's murder. The possibility that he committed suicide came to mind. There had been a space heater in the shed with my dad, and we wondered if it malfunctioned and poisoned him somehow. The people I knew who had died, died in accidents or in hospital beds. I couldn't recall a story where someone I knew had died at home like my dad did.

The dynamics of this type of death struck me as odd. It reminded me of Alexander's birth. He was very sick when he was born, and the nurses and doctors whisked him away from me shortly after he arrived.

Days later, Dan and I held Alexander for the first time. Even though he was ours, he wasn't really ours. It felt like he belonged to the hospital. I felt so powerless and completely at the mercy of the doctors and nurses who so swiftly and competently—thank God—had cared for him. I felt the same sense of powerlessness when the police officers urged my mom to leave my dad, and the coroner took pictures in the shed. I would love to know what the coroner captured that night. I wonder what he was thinking and what became of the pictures he took. It is strange, yet slightly reassuring to think that, for the coroner, it was just another night on the job.

Officer Greg knew that we wanted Sarah to have the opportunity to see my dad before he left. The coroner had been running late and was anxious to leave once he finished his job. It was getting really late, and there was the unimaginable aftermath of a bad traffic accident he needed to tend to.

Minutes after Sarah arrived at the house with her husband and baby daughter (in their own car), we stood on the front porch as a stretcher moved from the backyard to the driveway. There was a large body bag on the stretcher, and even though I knew what was happening, I could not conceive of the reality that it was my dad's body in that bag. In the same way that Alexander had been mine at birth, but not mine to hold, my dad was ours, but no longer able to hold us. I tried to remind myself that the body, my dad's body, wasn't really him anymore. Even so, I was developing a deep attachment to my dad's body. I wanted to keep it with us.

Officer Greg convinced the coroner to open the bag so that Sarah could see my dad. He looked so peaceful. We each touched his cheek, kissed his forehead, and wished him well on his journey. Then they took him away.

Wondering

I am standing at a podium in front of the room. We are at my dad's memorial service. My hand shakes as I open the small journal where I had written my thoughts about what to say.

My dad's voice says, "Anna, your hand is shaking! Did you eat breakfast?"

I smile, appreciating that he notices little things like my shaky hands and cares enough about me to inquire about whether I had breakfast. The voice is, of course, in my head. I stop smiling.

The eyes meeting mine are sad ones. Some of the eyes have been watching me my entire life. Some I have known since I was a child, some I met in college, and some I have never seen before. I hadn't planned on saying anything at all. I had imagined myself sitting there, nestled into one of the comfy sofas with my back turned to the people who came to say good-bye to my dad. My shoulders would be trembling, draped in Dan's strong arm. That was how I pictured it. Instead I stand at the front of the room, facing all those eyes I want to avoid.

I say, "Thank you for being here to celebrate my dad's life. None of us was prepared for this loss—especially my dad.

"There were many things he still looked forward to doing. And there were many, many things I looked forward to sharing with him, especially with him and my children. I cannot wrap my head around the reality that they will never find comfort in their Papaw's arms again.

"In times like this, my dad is a great source of comfort, wisdom, and strength. So, I am wondering, what would he say to me now? What would he say to all of us today? Would he say, 'Yeah, man. I died too soon. I left an unfinished life.'?

"Honestly, he would probably say, "Anna, life is not about finishing; life is about the process." Because that is how he lived his life. He relished in the process. He trusted in the process. And because of that, because of his quest to learn, to share, and to create, because we have his music, his art, and our memories to sustain us, we find ourselves not only lost without him but also always with him. We are surrounded by his love, his grace, his strength, his beauty, and his wisdom.

"All of his love, the love he gave so freely, is reflected in your eyes. For all of this, for his full, rich life, for my dad, I am grateful.

"Thank you."

I hear laughs when I impersonate him with my "Yeah, man." I cry through the entire thing. My knees are shaking along with my hands, but I make it through to the end of what I had written.

In the days after my dad's death, we are surrounded by love. We receive flowers, plants, phone calls, cards, e-mail messages, and text messages. None of it is expected. How could it be? We don't know what to expect. This is a new twist in the road on our journey. We took an unexpected turn. And, much to our surprise, our chief guide is no longer with us. We wait for him to walk through the door. We want him back so desperately. We saw his body taken away, and we know he isn't coming back, but we don't stop hoping. We have watched too many soap operas. People always come back from the dead in soap operas. The line between what is real and what we imagine begins to blur. It is all a dream. Yes. No? We can't really be sure.

We appreciate all the love whizzing and whirring around us. We feel blessed. We light up upon seeing people we haven't seen in so many years, and then we remember why we are seeing them. Could it be true? Has there been some sort of cosmic mistake? We hope so. We continue to greet our loved ones and the ones who loved my dad with half smiles. We nod to acknowledge those we can't talk to right away. I repeat the words from the script I pieced together for the occasion: *No, he wasn't sick. Yes, it was all of a sudden. My mom found him. Dinner was on the stove. He didn't come in when he was supposed to. Yes, it was awful. She is okay. I mean, she will be okay. She is strong. Yes, James was devastated. Yes, they were very close. It was an aortic dissection. His heart broke. Literally. It's good to see you too. I mean, well … yeah.*

I force my mouth to form a smile, but it is still hard to look people in the eyes. I hear my dad's voice whispering,

"Eye contact, Anna." But making eye contact means seeing and being seen. I try to avoid it. My head is nodding while my heart screams in disagreement with what is being said: *No! He is not in a better place. This is where he is supposed to be. There is no better place than right here. With us. Have you lost your fucking mind? No! It was not his time. He is sixty-fucking-two. Are you fucking crazy? No, this is not God's plan! It was an oversight. God made a mistake! Apparently that happens sometimes!* I take notes and file them away under What Not To Say To People When Their Loved Ones Die.

I am thankful for Spanx. I hate high heels. I wear them anyway to appeal to the southern gentleman my dad once was. I am a good daughter.

One of my very dear friends, Tiffany, is there, talking to people for every bit of the visitation. When I asked her about it later, she said, "I just wanted to be there. In case you needed me."

Another friend, Angi, hands me a Peppermint Pattie when I see her. It is the sweetest, simplest gesture. She said, "I thought you might be hungry."

The music we prepared is playing on the sound system. One of my dad's songs, "Nothin' But Love," is the theme song. Even in the midst of well-intentioned but ill-received platitudes, we are experiencing love in ways I never imagined. The love is thick in the air. It covers us like a blanket, protecting us and warming us. We are somewhat invincible cloaked in this love. We can handle anything.

The lyrics of my dad's song are as follows:

If you've never had the blues, you've got some blues coming,

If you've never had the blues, you've got some blues coming,

You might not be singing 'em, but you'll be hummin' 'em.

Ain't nothin' but love can take your blues away, ain't nothin' but love can take your blues away.

You might not live to see tomorrow, better make some love today.

You've got some blues coming, you know it will be hard.

You've got some blues coming, you know it will be hard.

It don't matter where you live, people, the blues'll come in your backyard.

Ain't nothin' but love can take your blues away, ain't nothin' but love can take your blues away

You might not live to see tomorrow, better make some love today.

—James Shields Hodges III

While I take comfort in his words, I wonder how he knew we had some blues coming? How is it that he wrote this song and then died in his own backyard? What other blues do we have coming? I think about the last recording my dad made. Every time I saw him after he gave it to me, he asked if I had listened to it yet. I said no. I didn't listen to it until after his death. I would give anything to go back and listen to it while he was alive. I would give anything to see his face when I tell him how much I love it—how much I love hearing him sing the blues. I relish the love that surrounds us and trust in my dad's reassurance that nothing but love can take my blues away. I am relieved that there is something potent enough to take my blues away.

A few of my closest out-of-town friends leave me kind voice mails. I don't even listen to them until weeks after the funeral. I save those messages and listen to them when I need comfort. I would save the messages for well over a year, and then eventually I would delete them because holding on at that point would be more painful than letting go. People make meals and run errands for us. We are at the heart of a huge and kind community of people who love us and want us to be well.

And then one day, it is over. The tangible love and support that cradles my mom, my sister, and me so tenderly—it fades away. I walk through Target, wondering how all these other people pushing their carts up and down the aisles can just go on with their lives when my life seems to have ended. I keep walking. Wondering. Wandering. Searching for solace in the eyes I meet along the way.

Reckoning

*D*an is back at work. The support system I have come to know and rely upon is officially dismantled. My mom is a widow. My sister lost her father. My dad slipped away. The people who have been rallying around us in the days after his death have turned their attention back to their own busy lives.

I am in the shower now. I am washing my hair. I rinse. As the shampoo suds fall from my head to my shoulders, and then down my front and my back, tears begin to fall too. Only a few fall at first. These are leftovers from yesterday and the days before. I thought I had cried myself empty, but there seems to be an endless supply of tears within me. They fall slowly but surely down my cheeks and disappear into the suds.

I think I am having a heart attack. Something like a gas pain strikes in my chest. The pain takes my breath away. I try to push it up and out with a burp, knowing it is something that must be released from my body. It is trapped though—just like a gas bubble only much more painful. I fall into myself, onto the shower floor, and I sob from the pain. It sounds like I am trying to exorcise a spirit from my body. This is an epic release—one that might have been in the making for years. Decades even.

Something like a safe is opening inside me. I wonder where it came from, and then I get the sense that I put it there. I was so very young when my parents told me my own beloved Papaw died. I didn't see him very often, yet we had a connection. When he and my Grandpa Jim came to visit from Texas and realized my parents were raising me with no television, they went out and bought one for us. It's the kind of thing only a couple of grandpas could get away with.

I have an old photo that I have kept near me since I left home for college. I am sitting on my Papaw's lap and wearing a pink bikini. The picture is black and white, but I know the bikini is pink because I remember it. My Mickey Mouse punching bag is next to us. Mickey is smiling, as always. Papaw's arms are wrapped around my waist, and his hands are folded in front of me. His pale, freckled hands look just like my dad's hands. As a young girl, I couldn't comprehend the loss of my Papaw. I wasn't familiar with the kind of sadness I felt. It was the first time I remember feeling truly at a loss with what was happening in my life. It was so similar to the way I feel now.

I was very young when I began to hoard and hide everything that felt uncertain to me. I locked my fear, confusion, and despair into a safe and kept it buried deep in my heart. This became my practice. I shoved my discomfort, my doubts, and my frightening feelings inside the safe as time passed. It was the place where I stored my life's most excruciating experiences. Those experiences raised questions I didn't know how to ask and they might not have had clear answers anyway.

By the time my dad died, there were many unresolved emotions and encounters stuffed inside that safe. There was the unwelcome sadness I felt when Papaw died and the sense of loss that followed the deaths of each of my grandparents. I watched with dismay as the branches fell from my family tree. I stored the terror I felt when my friend Courtenay was killed in a car accident right before our sophomore year of high school and the confusion that followed too many other losses—all lives that ended too soon. I didn't understand how a healthy child could die in a tragic accident or become ill and die. The safe was where I stored the pain I never processed. Nobody knew I carried such deep, aching, heart-wrenching pain with me.

By the time my dad died, the safe was full. In the shower that day, the safe in my heart burst open. Pain and anguish erupted out of the safe like a volcano and gushed out from the pit of my stomach to the base of my throat. There was sadness and anger and fear and shame. I wailed. I wept. I cried until I could not cry anymore. I caught my breath. I sighed. More tears, more sadness, and more aching pain surfaced. It seized the opportunity to escape—no longer able to hide in the shadows of my heart. I wondered if I would ever stop crying. There did not seem to be a way to stop.

Grief is an instigator. Grief shows up like a bully. Grief gets in your face and says, "Whatcha gonna do about it?" You can walk away, stuffing the pain into the depths of your heart and soul. Or, you can face Grief. You may even let it have its way with you. You may choose to let Grief transform you.

In the wake of my dad's death, my load was heavy. I was weighed down by thirty-seven years of grief and shame and guilt and fear and confusion. All of that and the additional burden I now carried, which was the burden of questions that would never be answered and the loss of experiences that would never be had, were too much to carry anymore. They broke me into pieces.

I stare into the face of Grief, its eyes searching deeply into mine. They search beyond the white and blue and the small black pupils of my eyes to the depths of my soul. Grief says, "Well? What's next?"

I cannot even fathom what could possibly be next.

I fly my plane on autopilot. Mindlessly, I make my way through my days just to get to bed so I can get up and do everything over again the next morning. Each day, I wake my children. Seven-year-old James doesn't like second grade. Four-year-old Alexander doesn't like waking up. Two-year-old Sophia more or less keeps sleeping. I dress the younger ones and help James if he needs it. I feed them, load them into the car, and drive to the elementary school to drop off James. We drive to the preschool and drop off Alexander. Sophia and I go home to play or run a few errands before we pick up Alexander a few hours later. We eat lunch together, the three of us. They make a mess, and I clean it up. Sometimes Sophia takes a nap.

We pick up James in the afternoon. I make dinner. They make a mess. I clean it up afterward. Sometimes Dan is there, and sometimes he works late. I wipe noses and butts. I read stories. And several times a day, I see a smile on one of my children's sweet little faces that stirs something deep inside me like an awakening. It is a reminder that I am living. With every smile I see or laugh I hear and every new trick I see one of my children master, I am replenished. These simple little moments inspire me to keep going. For a few seconds, I forget that I am on autopilot. I fly free. I land my hand on a soft little belly for some tickles or my lips on those precious little cheeks for a kiss. I close my eyes and feel those squishy little arms around my neck in a hug, and then someone cries, and I remember it is time to tuck them back into bed for the night so we can do this all over again tomorrow.

I am married to a man I love, and together we are committed to parenting our three healthy children. We live in a beautiful home in a nice neighborhood in a sweet little town in Michigan. We are healthy. We are living the dream. But I am not truly living. I work hard to maintain the façade that everything is as perfect as it looks from the outside. I feel like a fake. I am a fake. Any day now, I will be discovered. I have carried this fear for as long as I can remember. From a very young age, I lived in fear that any day the walls would come crumbling down around me.

My prophecy came to be the night my dad died. I looked at his empty body, and there were no signs of life. My first and longest standing support system was reduced to half of what it had been.

I look into Grief's deep, dark eyes, still not knowing what is next. I am unable to imagine how to repair the crumbled foundation that held me. I see the beautiful blessings in my life. I still have my husband and our kids. My dad, the one person who I never seemed to disappoint, was gone, but I still have my mom and my sister. They are also shattered and sad, but we made it through the most trying days of our lives together. We still love each other, and we have made it clear that we want to support each other through whatever the coming days hold. Grief taunts me. Grief calls to question what I believe to be true about it. Grief holds up a mirror to reflect back to me my life on autopilot. I question whether the life I see is the life I want to lead.

As the light shifts, creating a glimmer in Grief's eye, I see a different aspect of Grief.

Grief isn't an instigator. Grief is not a fighter. Grief is not a captor. Grief might even be a liberator. Grief begs me to heal what has not been healed. Grief beckons from the darkness to be disempowered. Grief is at my mercy; I am not at its mercy. Grief is an invitation to mourn the loss of what meant so much to me and to create new meaning—new life.

Grief does not keep me in bed each day, wondering how to go on burdened by its weight, worrying about my mom, and hoping that Dan and my kids somehow figure out how to take care of themselves.

Grief looks at me lovingly, as an angel might look at a small, lost child and says, "Anna, dear one, it is time to pick up all the tender pieces that have been unearthed from the depths of your soul. You are not broken like you think you are. No, sweet child, you are whole. But you are hurting. As long as you continue to hold your pain tight, to hide it, and to ignore it, your pain will continue to weigh you down and hold you back. It is time for you to heal the wounds you have carried in your heart. It is time for you to release the pain. It is time for you to grow."

Grief is kind and beautiful. It is bold enough to sweep right into my life, unwelcome and unwanted, and gracious enough to help me heal while it is here. It is inviting me to transform.

I look Grief squarely in its wondering eyes and say, "I'm all in."

Searching

Each morning, as I open my eyes, I wait for that sense of relief that comes after waking from a nightmare. I wait for the sleepy recognition that what happened while I slept was merely a dream. I thank God it was just a dream. And then, I realize my mistake. I remember that hearing my mom scream my name from my dad's shed in the middle of a dark, rainy night was not a nightmare. I remember my dad's empty body. I remember the images that haunt me from the night of my dad's death are real. I remember it actually happened.

I know other people survive the loss of loved ones. Some of the other people are my very good friends. I hadn't pictured myself in this position so soon. I knew it would be awful when I lost one of my parents, especially as I saw them embrace their roles as grandparents with such wide, open hearts. They adore their grandchildren. I never imagined how awful it would be to lose a parent. I had no sense of what that kind of loss would mean in my life. I was not prepared for the feeling that came when I realized that my very first support system had been dismantled—that I could no longer rely on it for reinforcement. I sit with these memories of the times where my worst fears were merely fears and wonder how this huge, unimaginable loss will affect me?

Before he died, my dad came to my house a couple times each week to watch Sophia and Alexander while I picked up James at school. I brought home muffins and coffee the day before he died, and we all sat around the kitchen table and ate together. My dad chose James's guitar teacher, Tim, and came every Thursday evening to take James to his lesson. He made sure James's fingernails were trimmed, and once the fingernails passed approval, they grabbed a snack from the pantry and left together.

James rode in the passenger seat of my dad's pickup truck, and they speculated on life's mysteries. They talked about aliens and Dan Callan, a local realtor who seemed to have the corner on the real estate market all the way from our house to the music studio. My dad jammed with James and Tim at the end of each lesson. At my dad's funeral, Tim shared that even though he hadn't known my dad for long, my dad would always live in Tim's soul.

James screamed when Dan and I told him that my dad died. He said, "Why? I didn't want him to die!"

I keep asking myself the same question: *Why? Why now?* I ask the question over and over as if knowing why would take my sadness away. I grasp for practical wisdom in the midst of a mystery. This is the way I make sense of the world and the way I always have. I ask why. Rarely are there adequate answers.

I cannot make sense of anything related to grief, but I know it has a lot to teach me. I allow it to explore my mind, my body, my heart, and my soul. Grief continues to push everything out of me. My body heaves while sobbing. My tears are cleansing the insides of me.

I notice a new look in Dan's eyes when he sees me. Where once he was sure, he is now doubtful. I start to feel sorry for Dan. He works endless hours at his job. He would do anything for anyone. He doesn't deserve a crazy wife. He needs someone to stand by him. He needs a wife who can adequately support him as he supports us and so many other people. I have a solution: I can rid him of the burden of a crazy wife. I imagine myself getting in my car and driving away. Our life together fades into a distant memory. He is laughing in the sunshine with our children. I am hiding in a hut somewhere in Mexico.

I come back to reality. I committed to walk with Grief, but I have no experience with grieving. For as long as I can remember, I pretended not to have feelings. I hid my feelings. I stuffed them deep inside and acted like everything was just fine. I am at a loss about how I can risk feeling the menacing feelings that keep rising within me. *I don't have the skills. I'm not equipped with the right tools.*

Dan always seems prepared for whatever life gives him. He is gritty. He is wise. He is resilient, and he never backs down. He saved me when I met him. We were both sophomores at Michigan State University, and I was a party-girl binge drinker. I look back at that time in my life, and I am sure it is only by the grace of God that I survived. Many nights before Dan were a blur.

I was dismissed from school after consecutive semesters of being on academic probation. I received my dismissal letter over the winter break, after the first semester of my sophomore year. My dad delivered it, unknowingly, cheerfully even, happy to have his family together for the holidays. I read it on my bedroom floor. I read it again. I panicked. I called my mom into the room, and within minutes, she was on the phone with my college. Never once did my parents suspect me of wrongdoing. That is one of the greatest blessings of being their child. I was the child of two love-crazed hippies, searching for something bigger and better than anything they had ever experienced in their lives. My sister and I were junior members of their search party. They parented us loosely and lovingly, and they believed in us and all we did. They were our biggest fans.

The day after I received the letter, my mom and I drove to East Lansing to meet with the man who sent it. My mom offered to come into the meeting with me, but I knew I had to go by myself. She waited outside. I didn't want her to hear me begging for another chance at college life because the driving force behind my desire to beg was the thought that I would rather die than be robbed of my opportunity to pursue a love connection with Dan.

Dan and I had our first real conversation over Thanksgiving break. We were sitting in a booth at Atlas Coney Island on Corunna Road in Flint. We were there with a group, but we sat together, tucked way into the inside of the booth, mostly alone even in the company of our friends. He told me he was Polish, and I dreamily thought, *This is it. This guy is my future husband.* My mom's parents were first-generation Polish. I loved being Polish. From as early as I can remember, I wanted to marry a Polish man. I did not want to delay the opportunity to get to know my future husband by being dismissed from MSU. As it turned out, I didn't have to beg. I was reinstated—free and clear to fall in love, and I suppose, to pursue a degree.

Dan has never had a drink of alcohol in his life. He jokes that I was out having fun until he came along. After I boarded the "Dan Train," the rest was history. The Dan Train travels at warp speed, and it rarely slows down. That is how Dan lives. Fast. Big. He works big, and he plays big. He was there for me in the days after my dad's death, arranging childcare and being present when needed or wanted, but eventually he had to shift his focus back to his job. I always knew that time was coming, but I dreaded it. I was a daddy's girl. I liked the comfort of a strong man by my side. I loved that it was Dan—the man who saved me from God only knows what when I met him and fiercely supported me ever since.

I wanted to rise up and out of my sadness for the sake of Dan and our children. I thought Dan deserved an attentive wife and our children deserved a mom whose head wasn't always in the clouds or crying into a box of tissues. Fresh from my dad's funeral and hearing the memories shared about my dad and his life and the way he touched so many people with his art, his music, his humor, and his kindness,

I knew better than ever that life is fragile. Life is precious. Filling it with people that matter and doing things that bring joy is a privilege. An honor. Life is an extraordinary gift. We, as humans, were put on earth to live our lives—not to cruise through them on autopilot as I had been doing for years.

I desperately wanted to be the girl who grew through adversity. As a full-time mom for almost eight years and now a sad one at that, I didn't know where to begin. I was so far removed from personal growth in my ongoing efforts to grow my children that I wasn't sure I even had the energy to focus on anything but them. I couldn't imagine adding an additional task to my to-do list, especially one as vague and daunting as growth.

I had already committed to working with Grief—to being open to what it came to teach me. I knew I had the option to make choices about where I would go from there. Would I stay in the dark, walking through life like a robot? Or would I make my way out of the dark and into the light? And if I chose that path, how exactly would that happen? How could I possibly come to grips with the reality that my dad was gone and the rest of us were to keep on living? The journey before me loomed ahead in the shape of a massive mountain.

I needed tools. I needed to become an expert in grief. I needed to study it, learn how to navigate it, and shop for the equipment I would need to climb the mountain. I needed guidebooks and road maps that would help me carve a route through my feelings. Entering each new phase of my life had felt a lot like joining a new club or taking on a new hobby. At first, my parents were my guides. They helped me get what I needed: tutus for dance class, high-tops for basketball, a fancy dress for the prom.

When I met Dan, we joined clubs together. We joined the First Job Out of College Club together. We joined the Marriage Club. And then, we joined the New Homeowners Club. And, eventually, we joined the Parent Club. I had to join the Lost a Parent Club alone. I had a deep desire to learn from Grief, but I had very little confidence in my abilities. I was so used to traveling in a pack by then—with Dan and our children—it was hard to imagine setting out on this journey by myself.

I didn't want to do it by myself. In some ways, I wanted to drag everyone around me down with me. I knew that wasn't fair though, and Dan couldn't do this work for me anyway. It was all on me to come to terms with the reality of my dad's death and all that this loss meant for me. I could let Dan support me while I walked with Grief—through my new reality—but that was about all he could do for me.

I headed to the bookstore, my favorite place to buy tools, with my mom. We cleared out the Death and Loss section.

Struggling

I am becoming fast friends with *On Grief and Grieving* by
Elisabeth Kübler-Ross and David Kessler. I carry it with
me everywhere I go. I am reading about the five stages of
grief: denial, anger, bargaining, depression, and acceptance.
I have heard about these stages, even studied them, but they
have taken on a whole new meaning for me. I learned that I
could expect to move through the five stages. I learned that it
wouldn't be a linear process. I learned that I might get stuck
and stay awhile in one stage or revisit a stage I had already
been through. I was suspect of the five stages. Five didn't
seem like enough stages.

In discussing other losses those who grieve have faced
in their lives, Ross and Kessler write, "What is left ungrieved
remains stored in our body, heart, and soul. It can come
out each time we experience loss anew." This resonates with
me. My own body, heart, and soul have spoken. All that was
left ungrieved inside me has made its presence obvious. The
losses I've encountered and the grief I buried deep inside
as a result of those losses is rallying to be heard, felt, seen,
and acknowledged. I've already decided to walk with Grief,

and even though I cannot envision how this journey will unfold, I've been gathering tools to help me. On some level, I am ready to grieve the loss of my dad and revisit what still needs to be grieved from my past, but I feel stuck before I've even begun.

While I remain open to the possibility that I can move through all five stages of grief and come out on the other side, the day-to-day struggles I face are still overwhelming. Getting my kids up and out the door every morning takes all I have on a good day. Doing the same thing while grieving seems nearly impossible. I wonder why time is so insistent on marching forward and why everyone around me is okay with that. I want time to stop. I need to catch my breath. I need to breathe.

I am failing at my job. I am impatient. In my darkest moments, I sometimes think that I don't want to even live my life anymore. It is too hard and I am too soft and I am not good at it. I am completely blown away by how much energy, patience, resourcefulness, and love it takes just to be a mediocre mom. It takes a lot. Before my dad died, I felt like I was under siege, like I needed a break, and like I was in over my head. Now I can't even imagine feeling that together.

My mom frequently visits my house because she doesn't want to go to hers. It is too painful for her. I wonder if the dinner my parents never ate the night my dad died is still sitting on the stove. She appears to be torturing herself asking, "What if?" and "Why didn't I? Her questions are natural and normal, I am sure, but I don't see how it can be helpful to keep asking them after a certain point. I want her to stop. It is hard for me to see her in so much pain, and I want to be there for her. I want to support her and my sister. I can barely talk to Sarah though. A crack in her voice is too much to bear. When she was younger and sad, I tickled her. I loved to hear her laugh. I could never stand to see her in pain. I hate that there is no way to protect her from her grief. Tickles won't make her pain stop. She also has to grieve. My mom has to grieve too.

I wonder if I have even begun the five stages of grief? I might be in denial. Could a person just stay there—in denial—forever? I am afraid to sit with every last feeling that surfaces from within my shattered heart. Grief is like a puzzle to me, and I am struggling to sort the pieces. I don't know how to clear the space and time to put the puzzle together—to allow these feelings to surface. I know the pain will keep wearing away at me if I continue to pretend it isn't there. I can't imagine allowing it to stay buried inside me until the next loss comes along.

I read and reread the words of Kübler-Ross and Kessler. I flip ahead in the book, seeking inspiration, and as I watch the unread pages go by, I see glimpses of all that I am missing. It becomes even clearer to me that the only way out of my sorrow is to move through it. There is no skipping ahead to the end. I really must sit with Grief and try to become her friend. I want to get to know her better. I want to hear her stories. I want to let her help me heal from mine. I must make space for grieving, and I must keep going at the same time.

This all seems impossible. James is fairly steady in his emotions and his ability to express them. Perhaps he is an old soul. Alexander can move from rage to bliss so quickly. Sophia is completely uninhibited and relies on me to react and respond to her whims accordingly.

On any given night, I stand in my kitchen. It is time for dinner. Dan is not yet home from work, and the kids are hungry. Our dog is hungry. My mom is here, and she is also hungry—even though she won't admit it. She is talking about transplanting things in her garden. She is afraid to turn on the air conditioner because she isn't sure how my dad rigged it each year. He did something with the something.

I am hungry too.

If we could eat our hunger, we would already be full. It seems like eons will pass before I can sit down and eat. They will need things before I sit down. James will be nearly finished by then. Sophia will be throwing her food onto the floor from her high chair. There will be meltdowns and dishes to be done. Settling everyone down for bed feels like planting seeds during a hurricane. Everybody is wanting. Each of us will continue to want something and struggle to varying degrees with how to express those wants.

I want to disappear.

When the darkness finally fills the sky and my babies have given in to nighttime, I will be ever so grateful that Dan is tucking everyone into bed. On the nights he isn't there, I will drag myself from bedroom to bedroom to say good night. When I kiss the boys, I close my eyes and inhale their boyish scents. I admire their freckles. I imagine that nobody will ever love them as much as I do. I save Sophia for last so we can cuddle longest. I will rock us both to sleep, drifting off as she does.

The enormous weight of the needs I fill for the people I love grows heavy upon my shoulders. I am afraid to stretch the tight muscles in my neck because I don't want them to kink up on me. I am nearly a hunchback.

When Dan and I finally settle into bed together, my eyes are heavy and closing. There is so much to say and never enough time to say it. There are plans to make and needs to express, and I will want to tell him all the funny things the kids said at dinner. If my eyes stay open, Dan might take it as a sign that I want to make love. I do want that, but not right now. I let my eyes close while he watches TV. He turns and removes my eyeglasses from my face. He places them on his nightstand. I rest so I can do it all again tomorrow.

Amidst these daily routines creeps a huge amount of unpredictability. Holding space for the randomness of grief while facilitating our day-to-day lives seems unlikely. It is safer, easier, to move through my life unfeeling or barely feeling. It has seemed essential. *Safer* has run its course; while I am reluctant, it is even more important to feel now. Maybe this is the stage of grief I am in. Even before denial, there is fear—and then leaning into the fear and allowing myself to feel my way around what lurks in the darkness.

I don't yet know that grace is somewhere between the stages of grief and surrendering to the road that paves the way through them. To face what I cannot predict and to feel safe in that process will require a great deal of grace.

There will continue to be shifting, falling, and rising as I learn to feel while I help my children navigate their feelings and their lives. Living and grieving will be done at once. Together—with Dan, the children, my mom, and my sister—we will move in and around these five stages. There are probably other stages too, but we will try to assemble the pieces of this cumbersome puzzle. I will come to rely on grace as I do my part, my work, which is to sort through what has accumulated—what was left ungrieved, or unfelt—in my body, heart, and soul.

Missing

I miss my dad.

Opening

My mission is clear: I am the phoenix, and I will rise up and out of the ashes. I cannot continue to waffle back and forth between moving forward and staying stuck. I will not shut down. I will excel at grieving. I will be Grief's best friend. I will feel everything that comes up for me. I will sit with each and every feeling, I will honor each feeling, and I will hold it for as long as I need to hold it. I will make intentional choices about what to keep and what to let go. I will transform my pain into beauty. I will learn, stretch, and grow in the face of adversity. I will grieve, be a great wife, a loving mother, a good daughter, and a supportive sister. I've got this.

I feel more like a swamp monster rising up out of the mud than a phoenix rising from the ashes. Grief plays in murky waters. Nothing is entirely clear. I'm not sure I have the chutzpah to move ahead most days. For me, grieving will be like learning to walk as a toddler or learning any new skill for that matter. It will be a series of steps forward, falling down, tumbling back, and maybe lying there for a while before deciding to get back up.

I am on a curvy path. I am frustrated when I realize there is no distinct end in sight. How could there be? My life is forever altered. No one could expect there to be a precise end to this process of discovering what it means to move forward without someone who I assumed would be here with me. How could there be an ending? Everything is different. Everything is changing. Everything will continue to change.

My mom, sister, and I are in my car in the parking lot at Northern Community College in Traverse City. We are waiting to go into the building for a workshop: Writing through Grief and Loss. I look across the parking lot and see a stout, balding man getting out of his car. He looks sad. *Widower,* I think. We gather our things, make our way into he building, and join the class of four other writers. I expected a room full of sad sacks, like us.

Kathryn, our teacher is from hospice. She asks what brought us there that day. Two of the other women don't even mention a significant loss when it is their turn to speak. They say they just like to write and they know Kathryn. They like Kathryn. *Bullshit,* I think. I decide they shouldn't be there. A third woman shares that her husband is dealing with hearing loss. *Humph,* I think. *It is awfully nervy to show up at a grief and loss class to mourn the loss of your husband's hearing while my mom sits here mourning the loss of her entire husband.*

By the end of the day, this woman would be the one for whom I would have the most compassion. As she shares her story over the course of our day together, I become sure her loss is the most devastating. It is even more painful and more significant than mine. This is the beginning of an ongoing game of questions and answers called What Would Be Worse? To lose someone suddenly or have a chance to say good-bye, knowing your loved one is suffering and dying? We who mourn the loss of a loved one know there are no answers, yet we cannot stop asking questions. What would be worse—to lose your husband or watch as your husband loses his hearing? I think I know the answer because I am already an expert in loss.

The woman's husband is a musician. My heart softens. She writes of her experience lying next to him in bed each night in silence. They are no longer able to connect, to talk softly before they drift to sleep like they had for so many years leading up to this loss. I cannot even imagine. Dan and I have our best conversations at night in the darkness of our bedroom when our children are tucked in. We sometimes giggle like two kids at a sleepover. He holds me. He listens to my stories and I listen to his. I cry into his chest when necessary. I cannot bear the thought of lying there next to him, unable to hear his voice or him unable to hear my voice. I still wonder about that woman and her husband.

The man from the parking lot is indeed a widower. Throughout our class, he continues to look sad and hopeless. He looks lost. He looks how I feel. He embodies grief in a way I can't allow myself to embody it. My grief has purpose. We are poised. We are on a mission.

Our first assignment is to write about grief triggers. As soon as I hear that, I want to go home. Writing is how I have made sense of the world since I wrote my first word though, and I know writing helps me work through things. I love the feeling of putting my pen or pencil to paper and moving it forward to organize the jumbled thoughts in my head. I love the sound my pens and pencils make as I write.

I decide to write about one of the first nights I was alone after my dad's death. Dan took the kids to James's Cub Scout meeting. I looked under the bed for my yoga mat and found the guitar my dad gave me before I left for college. It was in the guitar case he carried his guitar in when I was a child. The case is hard and gray with black trim, and my dad had drawn on it with a bold-tip black marker. A Sharpie maybe? There is an eye. And there is a symbol for yin and yang, a symbol that always fascinated me.

I traced each mark with my finger, wondering what my dad was thinking when he drew it on his guitar case. He would have been a young dad in love with his wife and his baby girl—and also a musician with big dreams. In many places, the guitar case was held together with duct tape. My dad was a master with duct tape. I had known the case almost as long as I knew my dad, and it felt like him to me. I opened the case, and a huge swell of heartbreak washed over me. His absence was so obvious. I felt the blues my dad used to play on his guitar calling out from my soul. I fell over the guitar case and lost myself to loud, ugly, uncontrollable sobs.

I wrote my assignment as if talking directly to my dad: I imagined you, your hands, pulling the duct tape, ripping it, carefully spreading it around the curves of your beloved guitar case. You loved duct tape. You used it for everything. I remember you taking your guitar out of the case when I was a little girl. It seemed like magic to me then—the mystery of the marks you made on your case and your ability to make music with your guitar.

As I sobbed, I longed for some magic. Where were you then with your duct tape? Could you conjure up a magic strip of duct tape to reassemble the pieces of my broken heart?

I wonder how I could possibly read my piece aloud in front of my mom and my sister when it was my turn to read? Would it break their hearts? Then I remembered that their hearts were already broken.

The most remarkable thing about broken hearts is that they are also open hearts. Broken hearts are soft and malleable. The locks protecting broken hearts have fallen to the floor—they are left unguarded. Broken hearts are easy to enter. Where the broken parts have fallen away, there is open space. Nothing is held too tightly anymore.

In the absence of what I took for granted before my dad's death—that my dad would be around for years to come—I am making new discoveries. My broken heart allows me to see the ways in which others' hearts are broken too. I am developing more compassion as others' suffering becomes clearer to me. I no longer wish to keep my pain stuck inside me. I want to get it all out. I want to break free from its burden, so that I may rise.

Exploring loss through writing allows me to externalize my grief—to get it out of me. Finally. Once I begin to open and release some of what I had held deeply and tightly for so long, I want to keep opening and releasing. No matter how hard and unpredictable this path is, I want to keep sitting here with Grief. It may even be that the longer I sit here, the higher I will rise.

Questioning

I t is early in the morning, and the babes need attention. I am tired, and my body is sore. I don't even want to open my eyes. I cannot muster the energy to make a fresh pot of coffee. I check the carafe, and it is still full from yesterday morning. I pour some into a Pyrex measuring cup and put it in the microwave to warm it up. I gross myself out with this desperate act to obtain a hot cup of coffee. I think I am the laziest of lazy—until I remember this is something my dad did all the time. He might save old coffee for days. Instantly we are bonded by a simple act of warming a cup of day old coffee. I welcome the coffee from the microwave and pour it into a mug. I sip, noticing how the coffee warms my throat and my chest. It warms my heart. I savor the bond formed over coffee.

And so it continues to be in grief—anything and everything can and will change in an instant. My thoughts and perceptions shift quickly now. It is a journey of up and down, back and forth, and ebb and flow. My only challenge is how to surf the waves that rise up to meet me. This is something I learn to expect and to embrace as truth. My only real challenge is to be present to what comes up for me in any given moment. I think I need some help with that.

To say I run high on the anxiety frequency would be an understatement. I was an anxious child. I am anxious adult. I was relieved in graduate school (a master's degree in social work) when I learned that an entire vocabulary exists to describe the ways I felt as an anxious, highly sensitive little girl. I learned that anxiety is real, and it was comforting to discover that I was not alone in my anxious thinking or the depressive thinking that often accompanied my anxiety.

After my dad's death, I wanted help soothing my wild, wandering mind, and even though I had committed to grieving what I had not yet grieved in my life, I wasn't sure how it would turn out. My feelings were more intense than I had ever experienced. My worries were more troubling. My obsessive thinking spiraled way out of control. I wasn't just sad; I was really sad.

I had a conversation with a friend about anxiety and depression. She said, "Anna, you don't have to live like this." She had been taking an antidepressant and felt much better than she had previously, but she was still able to feel her emotions. Taking some kind of medication to help ease my symptoms seemed like a reasonable step to take when I considered the challenge I faced of keeping up with my life while also grieving. I made an appointment with my doctor to discuss my options.

At that point, roughly two months after my dad's death, I was still uncomfortable being vulnerable. I was still absolutely uncomfortable showing that I was vulnerable. I may have even been ashamed of feeling so raw, so exposed, and so unstable. It wasn't comfortable or desirable to feel like I did, and it didn't seem acceptable either.

As a student of anxiety (and social work), I knew exactly what to say to leave the doctor's office with a prescription for an antidepressant without exposing too much of myself to my doctor. Over the years, I had completed numerous online questionnaires to confirm my anxiety (while online questionnaires can sometimes provide valuable insight, I wouldn't recommend using them to try to diagnose yourself). I rattled off a list of sure signs and symptoms of anxiety and depression. I shared that I had always been anxious. I answered some basic questions, and I left with a prescription for Zoloft.

I didn't like the idea of adding any extra chemicals to my body, and I was nervous about side effects, but I was desperate for help and was willing to try Zoloft. Before I visited my doctor, I would have said that taking an antidepressant was okay for my friend or anyone who needed to do so, but I was glad I didn't need to do it. It was a double standard, one of several ways that my actions were not aligned with my so-called beliefs.

After a few weeks, when the medicine seemed to be working, I was grateful for the relief it provided. The constant buzz of obsessive worry and doubt in my head faded dramatically. I almost didn't hear it at all. I couldn't believe that people actually lived like that—without obsessive thoughts running through their heads! I felt free. I didn't feel drugged or hazy. I felt just like me, only clearer. It reminded me of the first time I wore eyeglasses. I was fifteen. As we rode home from the optometrist, I stared out the car window in complete awe of all the sights around me, taking in things I could finally see clearly, things I hadn't seen before. I didn't know, for example, that I was supposed to be able to see individual leaves on tree branches. My vision had been blurry, but I didn't know any better.

I had the same sense of awe as I began to move through life with less fuzz in my head. I could actually focus on a conversation without falling off track and into my own inner world. I felt calmer than I could ever remember feeling. I still felt a full range of emotions. I could still grieve. Before I began taking the medicine, I was afraid it would numb me, and I was relieved when that wasn't the case. The Zoloft actually seemed to create some space for me to explore my feelings without all the anxious thinking I had been experiencing.

I knew that medication works best with therapy. I considered joining a grief group, or something like that, but I didn't feel like I had it in me to sit and listen to other people's heartaches. And I didn't have *time* to sit and listen to other people's heartaches either. Frankly, I was tired of sitting and listening. It is what I had always done best. I wanted to talk. Once I could actually separate my anxiety from the rest of what I was feeling, I was ready to go deeper. I wanted to be heard.

I searched the Internet for local grief therapists and found a woman in a neighboring town who looked kind in her psychologytoday.com photo. When I met her for the first time, I felt comfortable with her. Noelle was soft-spoken and kind. Her long, flowing skirt and turtleneck sweater coupled with her turquoise jewelry and sensible shoes led me to believe that she was a former hippie trapped in more conventional times, like my own mom and dad. She was a spiritual woman who was studying to become a shaman and open to just about anything I threw her way. I couldn't believe I'd found her in Livingston County, Michigan. She seemed a little out of place there, which was exactly how I felt, and we seemed to hit it off well.

Noelle helped me make connections between my reaction to losing my dad and what types of grief I had experienced, but tucked away, throughout my life. Ross and Kessler say, "As the pain emerges, we find new ways of healing ourselves that may not have existed before. Return visits to old hurts are an exercise in completion, as we return to wholeness and reintegration."

I told Noelle how Alexander had been whisked away immediately following his birth. He was very sick with meconium aspiration when he was born and could have easily died. Once deemed healthy, we brought him home, Dan went back to work, and I set to the business of mothering two sons instead of just one.

I often wondered if it is really true that all is well that ends well. It seemed like being grateful for Alexander's health and homecoming was the right thing to be. I didn't have the time or the strength to revisit the trauma of expecting a healthy son and giving birth to a sick one. I didn't know that would be necessary. I knew that we were so incredibly blessed and lucky to be welcoming a healthy, new baby to our lives, and I did what I thought any good mother would do: I tucked away the shock and heartache I experienced around Alexander's birth.

Just by telling my story to Noelle, the trauma I held from that experience began to lose its hold on me. I laid it all out there. I was scared when Alexander was born ill. Terrified. I was scared he would die, and I was scared that I couldn't handle the death of my child. I was scared that if he died, it wouldn't matter to anyone but me because he was only an infant anyway. I was scared that nobody else would get to know Alexander like I knew him from the months he spent exploring my belly. He was fierce. What would the world be like without knowing his fierceness? I was scared that if he lived, he would be forever scarred by the impact of not snuggling up to his mother's chest to nurse immediately following his birth.

The giant clots of blood coming out of my body scared me. My physical body seemed as traumatized as I was emotionally by the birth and by not receiving adequate rest afterward. Once Alexander came home—seemingly healthy—I worried about the long-term effects of not being held by his parents for several days, of being hooked up to wires, of a medically induced coma, of an ambulance ride between hospitals. There was so much to worry about.

I was worried about James and how he was adjusting to life with his new baby brother (fine). I was worried about the impact of having a new person in our family and how that would shift the dynamics of our existing family relationships.

I was worried about all the typical things a new mom worries about and felt scarred by my experience of Alexander's birth. As each worry and fear arose, I stuffed it. I kept myself busy.

In the stories I revisited with Noelle, I recalled how I was often told that I was "too sensitive" when I voiced my feelings as a child. When one of my parents said I was too sensitive, I felt like an oddball. I felt like I did something wrong. I *am* extremely sensitive. I grew up believing that was one of many things that were wrong with me. I took people's negative reactions to my sensitivity to heart. I came to believe that I would be better off hiding my feelings. It is heart-wrenching to look back at myself as a child whose response to feeling invisible was to go deeper into hiding. I felt a great deal of shame for even having feelings. Learning to hide my feelings saved me from further hurt. Eventually, hiding my feelings turned into denying my feelings as if they didn't even exist. That was how I learned to cope, and it was the only way I knew to cope with my grief. It explained why it was so hard for me to let myself feel, and consequently, to grieve.

In the months after I lost my dad, the feelings that came up for me were way too overpowering to deny. I knew I had to allow myself to feel those feelings no matter how uncomfortable they made me. I had dealt with my feelings by hiding them, denying them, and trying to pretend they didn't exist for so long. I was still too scared to let myself feel them. I had no idea where feeling my feelings would lead.

With Noelle's help, I began to rewrite the stories I had been telling myself for so long. I entertained the possibility that some of the things I had come to believe about myself were no longer true. I began to see my sensitivity as a gift. I began to trust that it was safe to feel what was left unresolved in my past and what was coming up for me after the loss of my dad.

One of my favorite songs as a child was "We're Going on a Bear Hunt." I am aware of different versions now, but then I only knew one. I remember sitting in a circle of friends. I was in preschool, and my teacher's name was Teddy. We sat Indian-style because we were born in the seventies (now the sitting style is called crisscross applesauce). Each of our knees touched the person's knees next to us, connecting us and making us one.

Teddy started the song by clapping each of her thighs with corresponding hands, and then she clapped both hands together—thighs, hands, thighs, hands. I loved the anticipation right before the words started. All of us in our circle had little smiles on our innocent faces, big eyes, and excited glances. Our bear hunt would begin at any second.

"We're going on a bear hunt," Teddy said.

"We're going on a bear hunt," we responded.

Thighs, hands, thighs, hands, thighs, hands.

"We're not afraid!"

"We're not afraid."

"Uh-oh! Grass! Long, tall grass!" Teddy's eyes were as big as plates. We were ready. We waited to make our next move as she said, "We can't go over it!"

"Can't go over it." We shook our heads back and forth, agreeing that we could not go over the grass.

"Can't go under it!" Teddy called.

"Can't go under it," we confirmed.

All together we yelled, "We've got to go through it!"

As we joined Teddy in making the motions for moving our way through the long, tall grass, we chanted "Swishy, swashy, swishy, swashy."

We made it through the grass and continued through a river, the mud, a forest, and a cave. When we found our bear, we ran all the way home. I loved going on a bear hunt.

As a family, we sang that song together on road trips. When James was a baby, my mom found the board book *We're Going on a Bear Hunt* retold by Michael Rosen and illustrated by Helen Oxenbury. She bought a copy and loved reading it to James. One day after we lost my dad, we discovered a parallel between the bear hunt and our grieving. Grief is like going on a bear hunt. When you come to the long, tall grass, you can't go over it. You can't go under it. You've got to go through it. In the same way, the only way I could see out of my grief was *through* it. Life is just one big bear hunt.

I told more stories to Noelle. As I spoke, the pieces of my broken heart broke into even smaller pieces. I wondered how that was even possible. I wondered how I could live with all the grief I carried. It was so much. It was too much. It was at times all-consuming. How could I even be functioning? How had I been able to function all this time?

Noelle said, "Anna, it sounds like you have learned to disembody."

What?

Noelle told me that people disembody to cope with trauma. I had learned it somewhere along the way too. It is a way of feeling separate from one's body and the pain it carries. As she explained the concept to me, a sense of knowing stirred inside my soul. I am disembodied. Much of the time, I am not in my body. I have disembodied for years to escape feeling my emotions and to escape feeling physical pain. I didn't know there was a word for it, but I might be a bit of an expert at it.

As a child, I disembodied when my parents fought. As a teen, I left my body at the unwelcome touch of a curious boyfriend. I disengaged from my body when I could not bear another suck on my nipple when nursing my children. I disembodied when their cries were too loud, too frequent, or too hard to hear. I checked out when people explained things to me as if I was a child incapable of understanding what they were saying. I disembody a lot. I could not remember the last time I felt that I was actually in my body. I had been operating outside of it for so long.

I missed my body. I wanted to be in it in all possible ways.

I worked with a favorite yoga teacher, Lee Ann, to learn more about the practice of yoga. I intensified my own practice with the intention of being present in my body. It helped a great deal. I knew I must be in my body to allow my grief to move through my body. I knew I must be in my body to feel the feelings I had resisted feeling for all those years.

I cried on my mat sometimes. Usually in child's pose. I didn't think anyone knew. My tears were between my body and me. My body thanked for me for giving it ways to process the emotions that had been stuck inside it. My mind was also freed through this processing and this movement. My body moved, and my soul pushed the grief right out of me like it was blowing air through a trumpet. *Deep breath in. Push grief out.* Slowly, I began to empty out the spaces occupied by stored grief. Again, I saw how this would be a lifelong process of taking in, acknowledging, and releasing. It would become another component of my practice. There would always be grief, and there would always be releasing.

It may sound morbid to expect that there will always be grief. However, I was beginning to see life as a series of losses. Loss is ever-present. Babies lose pacifiers. First graders lose teeth. People lose jobs. We break up with people. We lose friends, and we lose spouses. We lose houses, opportunities, and things we hold dear. We can choose to sit with the emotions stirred by these losses—or we can pretend they don't exist. We can take it all in, examine it, and let some of it go—or we can keep it inside and let it stay stuck in our bodies.

I am constantly struck by how all the pieces of me are connected: my mind, my body, and my spirit. I imagine that to recognize an emotion like sadness—knowing it can break me and I can rebuild—helps me further integrate mind, body, and spirit. My body works together with my spirit to feel, to connect, to dance, to run, to stretch, to experience pleasure—all the things my spirit cannot do alone.

With help, I am softening into the potential of my new stories and these new truths about who I really am: a sensitive, sometimes anxious woman who would do just about anything for a quick cup of coffee.

Reconciling

I am flipping through photos on my computer. Scroll. Click. Scroll. Click. Scroll Click. I want to find a good picture of my dad and me. None of the photos capture what I want to see. I'm looking at vacation photos. My mom, my dad, my kids, and I are in Leland, a small fishing town in Northern Michigan that my dad loved. We are posing by storefronts. There are pictures of us smiling at the camera. In a few, the kids are looking off in different directions. There is one, finally, that appears to be a good one: my dad and me on a bench with my three children. He is wearing an orange canvas shirt from L.L. Bean. The shirt is lined with brown plaid flannel. This could be the photo I'm looking for.

The seemingly perfect image blurs as I remember how my dad and I had a huge fight on that trip. James and Alexander were being loud while my mom and I made dinner, and I couldn't quiet them. They were two little boys on vacation in the summertime—in an unfamiliar place with very few props from their everyday life around to support them. I didn't even really want them to be quiet. In my mind, they could be as loud as they needed to be.

My dad made a comment about my lack of mothering skills. I lost it. I could not believe he had the nerve to criticize me. Looking back, I know he wasn't criticizing me as much as he was pleading with me to keep my boys quiet, just as he had begged my sister and me to be quiet when we were little girls. But in that moment, hearing his scorn, I felt like a little girl again. I felt shamed. I felt silenced. I wanted his approval. I wanted my dad to accept my children and me just as we were in that moment and as soon as I knew that wasn't possible for him, I exploded. All the things I could never say to him as a child erupted from my throat and out of my mouth. He was already planning to leave the next day and threatened to leave that night instead. I felt stuck between two acts of betrayal: betraying my dad to defend my children or betraying my children to appease my dad.

My rising emotions made it impossible for me to know what was a fact and what was my interpretation, what he really said and what I thought I heard, what he meant and what I imagined. It was so typical. We were repeating our family's lifelong pattern of arguing because we didn't know how to express our needs—because we were too scared of being rejected by the other to speak our truths. These arguments were seeped with emotions that couldn't be expressed, and therefore, they were always explosive. We were so lost in our own hurt feelings and the assumptions and misunderstandings that followed that we had no capacity for logic, compromise, or compassion. Only rage.

I had found the idyllic photo I was seeking, but I struggled to reconcile it with the story the photo didn't tell: It was not an idyllic vacation. I didn't always have a peaceful childhood. There were things that happened as I was growing up that impacted the relationship I had with my dad as an adult.

There was so much guilt attached to every unresolved argument we ever had. I began to question every aspect of our relationship. Doubt walked hand in hand with my grief. I wondered what I should claim as my own responsibility and what could be laid to rest with my dad. I felt like I was left with a legacy of misunderstandings, but at the same time there were many moments, both captured and not captured, where we were at peace and where we had fun together. In those times, only love shone through.

While acknowledging the heartache from my past, it was only the love I wanted to be left holding. That, again, would require a great deal of deconstructing stories, assessing the stories for truth, releasing what wasn't serving me well, and keeping what would help me heal. I was still tempted by the swiftness of one big sweep that could push all the discontent under the rug as if it had never happened. I was ashamed of the reality that so much was unresolved both from when my dad was alive and after his death. The only way I had ever known to deal with shame was to deny it—to pretend that everything was okay. I was also exhausted from playing that game for so long. I was willing to go through whatever was necessary to be left with love.

I knew that the act of pretending could be devastating. I knew there had to be another way. My dad was twenty-five and my mom was twenty-one when they married. I was born six months later. I now imagine them as two young, dreamy-eyed hippies over the moon in love with one another. While I am sure they were frightened by the prospect of becoming parents, I think they were also eager to welcome a new baby into their hearts and to begin a life together. They moved away from their families in the greater Detroit area to a smaller town about fifty miles away. They were approved for an FHA loan and used it to buy a house on a dirt road named Webberdale in what still seems like the middle of nowhere.

I didn't always feel close to my parents when I was a kid, especially after my sister was born when I was six. Even when my mom was right there beside me, she seemed to be hundreds of miles away. Now, when I look back, I can see my mom as a smart, inspired young woman who had started her own family and had her whole life ahead of her. She was taking college courses and must have been thrilled at the opportunity to study topics she thought were important and interesting. Like me now, she too was balancing. Her attention was torn between a potentially bright future ahead and the family in front of her. My dad was most certainly away, whether or not he was sitting in close proximity. He was either at work somewhere in the Detroit area, miles away from home, meeting friends in bars after work, or getting high in our living room.

My dad's pot was our "family secret." As a little girl, I watched as my dad carefully separated the "seeds" from the "grass" and rolled his "numbers." When he was finished, he put away his "stash," tucking the small sheet metal container out of sight beneath his chair in the living room and reminded me not to tell anyone about it. In elementary school, probably in the course of a lesson on just saying no, I learned that marijuana was illegal. With my wild imagination, I imagined a posse of cops banging down our door, finding his stash, and dragging my dad away. As an already anxious kid, the fear that my dad would get arrested and taken away for smoking pot gave me one more thing to be anxious about.

My cousin and I used to huddle in her basement, plotting different ways to steal our dads' pot and flush it down the toilet while they got high upstairs. In high school, I finally confessed to one of my friends that my dad was a pot smoker. I thought I was revealing a deep, dark secret. My friend wasn't at all surprised because she thought my dad was a hippie and therefore, naturally, a pothead.

My efforts to conceal my dad's habit from my friends were in vain. Somehow they knew. They said things like, "Of course your dad gets high, Anna!" Some thought it was cool. Some thought *he* was cool. While my dad smoking pot may have never really been a secret, I still carried the weight of having to treat it as one. I never quite knew how to let that weight go or even that it was a burden I no longer had to carry.

There were other secrets too. One summer I learned that one of my uncles was actually my half brother. My mom gave birth to him a few years before she met my dad, and my grandparents decided to raise him as their child. I was also told that on my dad's side of my family, my grandfather's long time "roommate" was actually his life partner. I felt betrayed. It was hard to understand how these two people, whom I knew and loved as my uncle and grandpa's roommate, were actually something else to me entirely—something that might have allowed for even deeper, more meaningful relationships. Not withholding the truths of who these people were to me could have made way for more sharing, more truth, and more connection between us. I would never come to know the stories behind the "secrets" because when I finally learned the facts and began to form questions, nobody was willing or able to answer them. What became clear to me was that when life gets complicated, we should pretend it is not. What I came to understand about reality is that we need to escape it. I learned that *truth* is a matter of perception. I learned not to trust.

I became accustomed to hiding the truth about myself. I thought it best to hide my flaws, my fears, and anything that might make me look undesirable to others. I did not grow up to become a deceitful person, but I struggled with my imperfections. I thought I had to hide them to be accepted. To cope with my discomfort, I adapted behaviors that allowed me to blend in with whatever was going on around me.

I never felt like I fit in, but I tried to make it appear as if I did. At least, I imagined that it appeared as if I fit in. I was the queen of pretend play. There were times I didn't even know what was real and what I had imagined. It was all a blur to me. No matter how hurt or angry or sad I was, I pretended to be happy. I smiled, I nodded, I was sweet, and I led people to believe that I had it all together. I doubted my place in the world, but I acted like I was exactly where I was supposed to be.

As I grew up, the stakes got higher. I got drunk for the first time the summer after eighth grade. I felt so relieved when I could stop trying so hard to hide my feelings. When I was drunk, I didn't feel responsible for anything. It was a time-out from all the trying and pretending and hiding; it was an opportunity to just be me. Little did I know, I was really only numbing my feelings, like my dad did with his pot and gin and tonics, and stuffing them even deeper into the depths of my hurting soul.

By the time I graduated from college, my efforts to appear as if I had it all together intensified. I was in a darker place than I had ever been. Dan and I broke up, and I was devastated. The future I had envisioned with him crumbled before my eyes. I had become so dependent on him to stabilize me that I wasn't sure how to function on my own. I had no money, no job lined up, and no plans for the future. I was petrified.

I moved to an efficiency apartment in Alexandria, Virginia, and worked for a nonprofit, making a measly salary with no benefits. I relied on my mom for a great deal of financial support. I was lonely and scared, and I didn't want anyone to know how hard it was for me. I walked the line between satisfaction in my self-sufficiency and bewilderment over trying so hard to be self-sufficient. I imagined that all my peers were completely self-sufficient. I spent less on groceries so I could afford to go to the bar. It was exhausting to pretend everything was okay when it felt so far from okay, but I continued to pretend. I think I was very good at it. I imagine that was the point in my life where that little safe inside my soul began to become really packed with the regret, fear, and shame that spilled out once my dad died.

Dan and I eventually reunited. We got married, and we were broke. I tried not to let on. With creative budgeting, we made it work. Those were some of the most enchanted times of our life together. We were struggling and working to build something together. Once we moved back to Michigan and had our first baby, pretending that everything was okay came naturally to me. At the same time, I was outraged by how difficult it was for me to be a mother. I had no idea it would be so hard to be at the mercy of someone smaller than my forearm. I didn't want to screw him up. While he napped, I read child-development books. I was frantic when James didn't act like the babies I read about and victorious when he did. I felt ill prepared and ill equipped for motherhood. I wanted to yell at my friends who had spoken so highly of newborns and motherhood. I thought they were insane. Not one of them had squeaked a word about what was true for me: parenting is hard work. I was grateful to find a few kindred spirits with whom I could share my struggles as a new mom, but I mostly suffered in silence, hoping I wasn't causing permanent damage to my baby and pretending I knew what I was doing (which actually isn't a bad strategy).

Beneath my fear that I was doing it all wrong was an even bigger fear that someone might think poorly of me because I was doing it all wrong. However, in the space I allowed myself for grieving after my dad's death, I let go of my concern over what people thought of me. My desire to grieve properly, to work through the five stages of grief, and to come out a better person required that I give myself grace to feel what needed to be felt without judgment. I came to understand that there wasn't a right or wrong way to grieve. It was only important that I grieved. Once I stopped judging myself so harshly, my fears about others judging me faded entirely.

Allowing myself to finally be honest about my feelings after my dad died was incredibly freeing. I didn't want to pretend anymore. I no longer held the desire to appear as if everything was fine when it wasn't. I even lost the desire to pretend something wasn't fantastic when it truly was. I no longer felt like I had to downplay what could be celebrated. I wanted to experience every feeling to the fullest extent possible. I wanted to cry and rage and howl at the moon. I wanted to live—to be fully alive. I wanted to be real—to be me.

Like almost everything I was learning as I grieved, remaining true to myself would require practice. I still struggle with some of the feelings that arise in tense situations. I sometimes want to pretend that everything is okay instead of sitting in my misery. I still think I might not be ready to hear the messages my emotions come to tell me. This sometimes happens when I'm having difficult conversations with my mom. There have been many times when I recall a memory from my childhood, and she flat-out denies that it ever happened. Either she is actually in denial, which is quite possible, or she doesn't remember what actually happened because really, who can remember anything when raising children? As I observed the absence of continuity in our recollections of the very same events, I saw very clearly how elusive the truth really is. I better understood how her truth about my half brother varied from his truth or my grandparents' truth or even mine. We each have our own stories and our own truths around the very same fact, and those stories are rarely exactly the same.

The elusive quality of truth makes it that much more sacred to me. I can only be absolutely sure of my own truths (I think we have many), which might even vary over time or depending on circumstances. With that surety comes a sense of responsibility to hold and honor what I know to be true for me. I have been hurt by so many lies in my life—lies of my own and lies told by others. Lies I told to myself and the lies others told about me. While I know that lying or even just pretending is a skill we learn to protect ourselves, I no longer need protecting that way. To deny anyone the freedom to show up and live as they are is unjust.

Even when it would be easier, I no longer pretend to have it all together. I admit to being a wreck at times. I actually like that I am a wreck. I love that I am flawed. I love to imagine this wild and limitless spirit of mine trapped in this human body—confined only by my humanity and tasked with the enormous challenge of life as a human. The opportunity to live is a great one. When someone we love dies, it is common to suddenly develop a new appreciation for life. I wish we didn't wait for that. Why not appreciate the big, hard, messy, real, ugly, and beautiful life we have now? Why not go for it? We have nothing to lose and so much to gain.

This is truly a softer, more comfortable way to live. I am open, fluid, and trusting where once I was closed, rigid, and scared. I think about the things that were left unsaid when my dad died—the arguments we didn't resolve, the apologies we never made, and the grace I never gave. I so badly wanted a second chance after his death—to make amends, to ask forgiveness, and to forgive. The weight of what was left unsaid, and what was once a burden to carry, is lesser now that I am open to feeling and grieving.

I am embracing my life experience in new ways. What has remained in the dark, mostly out of fear, once haunted me, and now it has lost its power. I still have fears, but I am learning to welcome my fears as messengers. Some carry insights along with them, and some are just irrational. I can decide which fears are valid and which have no basis in reality. I recognize now that, just as was the case with my parents and me, my children, Dan, and I are all learning and growing up together. It's okay to go all in, to make mistakes, and to make adjustments as necessary.

From this vantage point, made clear to me only by Grief, I see with much more clarity. No matter what my parents said or didn't say, I trust they were doing their best. I know they loved me. Being true to myself now is all about choosing to open my arms, my mind, and my heart to that part of the picture. Instead of feeling embarrassed, guilty, or ashamed about any part of my life story, I can acknowledge the pain and the reality that life can be hard.

We're all doing our best, and it is safe to trust in the love that is always present. By embracing the truth in my story and not denying it or trying to hide it, I am completely free to show up exactly as I am—both in sadness and in joy. I am free to choose to see the love in the bigger picture, even when it is, at first glance, clouded by the confusion that can arise from experiencing life as a human.

Strengthening

Even as I am beginning to expect the unexpected, I continue to struggle with the unpredictability of grief. I can be feeling upbeat, but then see something like a dad walking with his daughter and I'm moved to tears. In the cases of dads and daughters or grandpas and grandchildren, I envy the physical connections I see being made.

Sometimes when I'm having a good day, my mom will show up with tears in her eyes, and that incites my own tears. Sometimes when I'm talking to Sarah on the phone, her voice cracks, and I feel my heart sink. Sometimes when I hear James playing the twelve-bar blues, I have to stop to catch my breath. I'm moved by pride and regret that my dad isn't here to nod his head along with James as he plays. Immediately following my dad's death, when I was walking around town in a daze trying to decipher my grocery list and wondering how everyone could just go on with their lives, these surprise surges of emotion would feel like daggers through my heart. Now they are more like pinpricks, but they still throw me off track. I wish they would make appointments.

I am frustrated sometimes. When I think I am making "progress" in moving my way through grief, these unanticipated reminders that there is no finish line feel like setbacks. A lot of people say that grief comes in waves, and that makes sense to me. It is inevitable that the waves will hit and that sometimes it will come as a surprise. I've also heard people say that the grieving process is like climbing a spiral staircase, as opposed to traveling a straight line. You may move up a few steps, and you might fall down a few the very next day. And so you continue—up and down indefinitely—maybe until the end of time.

I wonder how I can be in the midst of a universal experience like grief and still feel so alone. I want to talk about my funeral, and nobody wants to listen. They think it is depressing. The party planner in me takes pleasure in daydreaming about the flowers and the music. I don't know why these thoughts pop into my head. Perhaps it is an indication of my longing to die relevant or leave a lasting impression. It is almost comical to sit as a witness to my own thoughts. It is like watching *Saturday Night Live*. I am constantly acting out skits in my head. Glimpses of my life experiences come full circle, and it is perhaps frightening to imagine the circles closing.

My mom is having her own experience, and I wonder if she is making it harder for herself. She seems to be keeping her home as a shrine to my dad, and that worries me. Dan and I spent the afternoon with her at my parents' house recently. She and my dad had a lot of interests, and they had a collection to go with each interest. They enjoyed exploring antique stores together. She searched for kitchen tools to add to her collection. She liked wire whisks and washboards. He liked saws and lanterns and pottery. As a musician, he had guitars, music stands, amps, and a microphone on a stand. He had sketchbooks and woodcarving and sculpting tools for the artist in him. Tools and duct tape for the handyman. Between them, they had hundreds of books to satisfy their appetite for learning and stacks of journals for writing. There is more. There is a lot of stuff. And now we have to figure out what to do with it all. This was unexpected, and it is an intimidating task. Perhaps a shrine makes sense after all.

His spirit lingers in all of his things. My dad once touched every tool, big or small, each and every book, and he wore just about every stitch of clothing. He wore some of his shirts and jeans thin. His scent is mixed up in all of it. A single strand of his long, silvery-white hair falls into my lap when I pick up certain pieces of his clothing. There was one on the red union suit I pulled from the pile. If we close our eyes, we can trick ourselves into thinking he is here. It is hard to know what to keep and what to let go.

My mom has a friend in her grief group who donated most of her husband's belongings when he died. It sounds like she never looked back. That would never work for my mom or for any of us. We are collectors, and my dad's belongings are part of our collection. They are seeped in memories and are the only hard evidence we have of a life once lived. All of his stuff reminds me that I still long to say good-bye properly. With a hug and a kiss. I want to look into my dad's eyes one last time. I want to hear him say my name.

As I tried to help my mom pack some of my dad's clothes in a Rubbermaid tote, I cried and cried. I wanted to wrap his corduroys around my neck like a scarf and curl up in a ball on the floor. The thought that his long, thin feet would never fill a warm woolly sock again was almost too much to bear. The silly T-shirts he collected through the years remind me of his dry sense of humor. One says "I (heart) Intercourse" in big letters (as in Intercourse, Pennsylvania). How could we possibly let them all go? Could we even choose just a few to keep around? What would we do with them if we did keep them? Would we really make a quilt out of them? Who would keep the quilt? We would have to make three quilts. At this point, it seems easier to keep it all in totes for a while. Maybe forever.

Watching my mom experience the loss of her husband is its own form of torture. Our roles are reversed sometimes. I look out for her more now. It seems like it has been so long since she has sheltered me, yet there has always been a sense of being safe at home when I am with her. That sense remains the same, yet it is different. The home is on shaky ground. It is shaky. She is shaky. We joke about this being our "new normal." The "new normal" is what we're supposed to be moving toward after loss. I think it is a fairy tale. The new normal is purely a mirage in the desert. Was there ever an *old* normal? Aren't all these waves and spirals just life? Aren't we always experiencing some type of loss and then trying to make sense of it afterward? Isn't life always unpredictable? Everything seems more intense now; it's like an exaggerated version of what always was. The only difference is this loss was not one I could ignore. This loss was like an earthquake, shifting the ground beneath me, bringing down the walls around me, and shaking me to my core.

It could very well be that my role at this time is to rally. Because while the earth is quaking and the waves are rolling in—and even while I stumble up and down the spiral staircase that is grief—I am waking up to the world around me. I am paying closer attention. The wound in my heart is not as raw as it was initially. It is not so tender to the touch. The pit in my stomach is growing smaller.

Occasionally, I see the world as if I am seeing it for the first time. I am appreciating things I had begun to take for granted: my children, my husband, our family, my mom. I always knew life was a treasure, but I forgot it as I flew through my daily routine. I love to slow down now, stare into my children's eyes where I see their souls, and pour love into them like the milk I fed them as babies.

I think I am beginning to understand what it means to lose a parent forever, with no hope of return. It's no longer possible that my dad stepped out for an errand when I realize he is missing at family gatherings, or that he is on a trip somewhere. He is gone. He will not come back. This makes me sad, and I miss him. However, when I see a picture of him now, I am starting to feel more and more grateful for having had a dad worth missing.

I'm beginning to open to the possibility that my dad is still here somehow—even if I don't prefer the form he takes now. And while grief is still new to me and rather unpredictable, I am finding peace in accepting it as just that.

I am releasing my tight grip on life and learning to trust in the flow. I am strengthening my heart muscles. I am flexing them to accommodate the quickly shifting demands of the heavy burdens and the lighter ones. These moments, which once seemed unbearable, are teaching me about the strength I always carried but didn't believe I had.

I now know that I am resilient enough to bounce back from the surprise sensations that rise in response to everyday life: a grandfather and his granddaughter, untouched piles of my dad's belongings, and the melancholy shadows of gray in my mom's blue eyes. I find my way back more quickly than before. I am growing more comfortable with the mysterious side of Grief. Grief still has surprises in store for me, but I know the blows can't take me down entirely. Eventually Grief will present very few wonders that I don't recognize— that haven't left me in awe once or twice already.

Honoring

I t is January, and in two months, we will have made it through our year of firsts. My mom and I are on our way to Sedona. Sarah will join us in a day. We wanted to take a trip to celebrate my mom's sixtieth birthday, but we weren't even sure where we wanted to go.

In a Google storm one day, I found a company called Sedona Soul Adventures. Within hours, we were making plans for our trip. It would entail a host of meetings with spiritual healers and practitioners for each of us individually and a day "on the land" together. It sounded intriguing, magical, and like the medicine we needed to move forward after a year of unexpected grieving.

It was dark when my mom and I finally made it to the winding roads of Oak Creek Canyon where we were planning to stay for the duration of our trip. Our "angel guide" at Sedona Soul Adventures helped us find this place to stay. We met our hostess, Ranjita, at the Wildflower Bread Company in Sedona so we could follow her to Your Heart's Home, her permanent home and our home for the week. On Ranjita's website, she says, "As with any pilgrimage to a sacred site, you will be entering onto the 'road less traveled.' This includes a 7/10-mile-long dirt road, which transitions you from the fast pace of your life into magical time and sacred space." That description could not be more accurate. Traveling the winding dirt roads up and down hills to Ranjita's home felt like taking our very own trip out of the birthing canal. It was like being born into the unknown.

In the light of the new day, I felt as if I actually had been delivered into something new: a new way of being that I had never experienced. With massive cliffs towering over us, like those I had only seen in photographs, it seemed like I had landed in a completely different dimension than the one I'd left the day before. I had heard that "the veil is thinner" in Sedona, that being there brings you closer to God, and while that sounded mysterious and impossible at first, as soon as we arrived, it was as real as the enormous Red Rocks of Sedona.

The week was filled with fresh, wholesome food, miracles, and everyday magic. Time expanded and contracted to meet our needs. I expected the healers and practitioners to unravel mysteries and tell me what I needed to change about myself to find peace and experience joy, but mostly they took me on journeys into my own heart and helped me see what was already there. What I saw was beautiful. They helped me embrace the reality that it had always been beautiful. All along, the contents of my heart were good and whole, and nothing ever needed to change. It only needed to be acknowledged and, eventually, put to use.

While we were there, we had the opportunity to perform a "Letting Go" ritual with a minister named Yana. We hiked a flat path along Oak Creek to Red Rock Crossing and sat in awe of the world-famous Cathedral Rock. We settled into an open space on a bed of large, flat rocks next to the creek. We prayed together. Yana guided us through a meditation and anointed us with essential oils. It reminded me of the chrismation in James's baptism ceremony in the Orthodox Church, when the Father dabbed him with the chrism oil and whispered, "Sealed," sealing him with the gift of the Holy Spirit.

In so many ways, our trip to Sedona was exactly like a baptism—a cleansing of our weary souls. We reflected on my dad and our memories, and we scattered some of his ashes. We each had our own handful of ashes to scatter. They were gray like any ashes, but instead of feeling soft and smooth, they were hard and lumpy where bits of bone remained. It might be hard to imagine, but the ashes were stunning. They glistened in the sunlight as we held them in our palms.

Sarah and I released our ashes separately and in our own quiet ways. Just thinking about it, my body remembers the peace I felt that day, in that moment, releasing my dad to the welcoming waters of Oak Creek. I will never forget the sight of my mom releasing her handful of my dad's ashes. As she tossed the ashes into the creek, she threw her head back and howled like a wolf—as if to unite our pack one last time. As we let go, we were inextricably connected to all of Creation, kneeling at God's red rock altar. These rocks, thousands of years old, sacred places of ceremony and reflection for Native Americans, exquisitely held space for us to conduct our own sacred ceremony. I could feel my heart mending as it beat in my chest, one with God, our earth Mother, and my original pack—my sister, my mom, and the spirit of my dad. I have endless gratitude for that opportunity.

Before we headed back to Michigan, one of the practitioners suggested that we share something similar with our children and the rest of our families. As the first anniversary of my dad's death approached, my mom and Sarah and I began to make plans, thinking about what we wanted to be sure to include.

We decided to hold our ceremony at our cottage in Northern Michigan. My dad loved "up north," and it seemed very fitting to honor him there. The three of us even became Internet-ordained ministers to help make our performance of the ceremony more "official." I borrowed excerpts from a few different books on blessings and rituals. I added my own words and came up with a ceremony where everyone present would be involved in honoring my dad. I hoped we'd also be celebrating each other and the lives we have left together. I didn't realize it when I was in the midst of it all, but all of the planning and crafting of words was very therapeutic for me. I like to think the same was true for my mom and Sarah.

I was set with our service, the guests, our dinner plans, and even the programs. I wanted it to be a celebration. I even invited my dad, informed by the knowledge I gained in Sedona: that life is busy even in the spirit realm. I wanted to honor my dad, but it was a lot like a birthday party for the rest of us. We had made it through our first year, the hardest year of grieving according to many, and that was something to honor as well. I envisioned a beautiful, sunny, albeit cold, day surrounded by loved ones on the shore of Lake Michigan.

Friday and Sunday were gorgeous. In between the two was the day of the ceremony, and as it turned out, the snowiest, coldest, most blustery day of the year. I asked if people wanted to stay inside, but nobody did. We all bundled up and headed out. The beach was really way too windy, but we set up in sweet little spot under a tree. It was not what I had envisioned, but in retrospect, the frigid cold and flying snow provided an apt reminder of the volatility of grief. Nature knows how to plan a relevant ceremony even better than I.

We read our parts and shared memories of my dad. We made an offering of stones to the land, and we poured a cup of strong, black coffee as an offering to my dad. My mom and my sister and I walked down to the beach to a large rock we'd all come to know as my dad's rock, and scattered more ashes. The landscape was different from Sedona, and the temperature was *very* different. The sentiment, the act of scattering, and the flowing water before us were the same, and they reminded us that the experience of loss, while painful and vast, is also small and perfectly natural in the context of the universe.

After we scattered the ashes, we joined the others who had already gone inside. By the fire, we toasted my dad and each other with champagne and homemade macaroons (his favorite cookie).

There are many ways to honor and remember lost loved ones. I read a story about a family whose mother passed away right before her seventieth birthday. They decided to have a "birthday" party for her and invited all her friends to share in a night of remembering and celebrating the woman they lost. I know there are also all kinds of memorial services based in religion and in culture that provide a similar sense of honoring the lives of those we loved and lost.

As individuals and in small groups, we do many beautiful things in remembrance. As a whole though, I don't see a lot of place for grief in American culture. It seems like we are more likely to suggest that the grieving "move on" or "get over it." It is hard to sit idly by as people we care about suffer. We feel helpless; of course we want them to move on. We don't like to see anyone we care about in pain, and we don't like to be in pain. Heartache would be a million times easier to handle if we could all just get over it.

In the year after my dad died, two of my very dear friends also lost parents. Even after losing my own dad and knowing everything I had come to know about grief and grieving, I felt helpless. I hoped those two women could find the strength to keep going. I hated to see them so sad, and at the same time, I already knew enough about how my own grieving process was changing me that I didn't want them to move on or get over their losses too quickly. I wanted my friends to give themselves the gift of grief. Sometimes, I think the most profound thing we can say to our grieving loved ones is, "Hey! I'm here." As excruciating as it was for me to be there, I wanted to be as present as possible for my friends.

In the absence of abiding by religious or cultural traditions, we have the freedom to create our very own ceremonies to honor loss. In ceremony, we celebrate those or what we've lost, each other, and what is to come. This is not an effort to get over it. It is a way of sitting with it and honoring our sadness for the gift it is: a reminder that what or whom we lost mattered. Merely sitting beside another loved one can be an exquisite ceremony in and of itself. For me, it was incredibly gratifying to find a way to honor my dad and the grief that surrounded our loss of him in our very own way.

In as much as I am grateful, I also dread what lies ahead. I feel like I've been living in a protective shelter this first year. I'm safe in a bubble that says, "I'm grieving and I'm fragile. Be gentle with me because I might break at any minute." I wonder whether the bubble will pop. I never thought I'd lose my mom or dad before they had the chance to watch my children grow, but now I know that death does not discriminate. It touches all of us at one time in some way or another. It hit me hard this time. I'm much more sensitive to the fact that it will hit me again. Sometimes I even catch myself holding my breath, fearful of what lies ahead.

Someone asked me if I was okay via text message recently. It took me two hours to answer because I didn't know what to say. I am okay. I guess I'm also holding on to the possibility that I am not okay—in case I crack or something. The truth is that I am okay and I am a wreck at the very same time. I know my dad is with me, and I miss him desperately.

While I celebrate making it through the first year of grief, I dread what comes next because the hard part is all I know. I'm afraid of what's to come. I didn't know it was possible to feel such conflicting emotions at once, but learning to negotiate the balance between these extremes is providing the juiciest opportunities for my expansion into living life more fully. It is a blessing to be all these things—okay and not okay, content and wanting more, grateful and fearful—at once.

Owning

Grief is challenging me to do many things differently. Right now, it is begging me to take better care of myself. Granted, this is something I will be called to relearn often. My own self-care is the first thing to go when I am stretched for time and energy. Taking good care of myself requires diligence and awareness, which are also the first things to go when I am stretched and trying to keep all the people and all the things moving in the proper directions. It is like holding my breath and going underwater. I hope to come back up. I have to trust my body to take me to the surface. I am at the mercy of my lungs and the water. This habit of going under is so well practiced that my cells remember to do when I'm not paying attention or being mindful. Developing an awareness that I could propel myself back up to the surface once I touched bottom requires unraveling more of the stories I have come to believe about myself and the world around me.

Piece by piece, I am examining my habits, my beliefs, and my expectations. I look at the stories I had written based upon all my experiences. So many of my stories begin in my parents' home. I took violin lessons in fourth grade. I learned "Hot Cross Buns." While playing that simple little song on my violin, I felt like a master. I reveled in my ability to make music with my bow by moving it against the strings on my instrument. The soft and lovely sound soothed my soul. I had no such feeling at my recital. Performing on a stage in front of people terrified me.

After the recital, I told my parents I never wanted to play the violin again. I never did. Years later, I began to wonder why they didn't force me to keep playing. I blamed them for not making me learn an instrument because I wished I could play one. The same thing happened with dance at my recital. I didn't mind acting in plays in elementary school, but my parents didn't help me pursue acting. As such, my failure to become a movie star was their fault. Obviously.

There are so many aspects of myself that I could blame on my parents. I blame them for my inability to stay with just one thing: my resistance to finishing it, my insecurities, my bad judgment, and my impulsivity. I wish they had picked up on my anxiety. I wonder how life would be different if I had been offered help. I blame them for all of my shortcomings. I do like myself though, so I can somewhat appreciate the trouble they caused me since it helped me become the person I am today.

At some point in my past, I cast myself in the role of victim. Before I lost my dad, I was still living my life from that place of powerlessness. I was blaming others for my inability to do or get what I wanted out of life. It's hard to say definitively when I developed that habit. I imagine a series of events led me there. Perhaps it started at one of my varsity basketball games in high school. I was a benchwarmer.

At an away game, my team's best players had boosted our score so far ahead of our opponents' score that the benchwarmers were allowed to play. I was an awkward mess on the court. I couldn't remember the plays very well, and since I had little opportunity to practice them under pressure, I was never exactly sure what I should be doing. Nonetheless, I loved playing basketball. I loved my coach and my team.

Since we were so far ahead, there was just one star player left on the court. She was a few points away from breaking a school record. With plenty of time left on the clock and a hefty lead, the benchwarmers were called back to the bench. It was crucial that our star break the school record for scoring. Of course, there was no possible way she could break that record with the benchwarmers on the court with her. At least, that was what our coach concluded.

One of my favorite friends (a fellow benchwarmer) and I took one look at each other when we got back to the bench and said, "Let's go." We stood up and walked back to the locker room. We had had enough. It seemed ridiculous to take us out of the game. Our coach's lack of confidence in us was evident, and it felt like being sent to my bedroom without dinner. It felt like being locked out. Rejected.

In the locker room, the two of us huddled together behind some lockers while our coach congratulated the rest of the team and our star from another place in the locker room. After the game, when all our teammates and the junior varsity team made it back to the bus, we heard our coach ask if the two of us had made it onto the bus. A few people said yes.

The athletic director called us down to the office the next day during school. We were given two options: Apologize to our team and be suspended from playing for two games (which was a bit of a joke since we didn't play much anyway) or quit the team. Never once did our coach or athletic director approach us with any kind of tenderness or grace. Never did they offer to help us navigate what they thought was a bad choice for us to make.

Two girls leave the bench in the middle of a basketball game, and nobody asked if we were okay? Anything could have caused us to leave the game. One of us could have been hurt or leaking blood from our adolescent bodies. They had no idea. They assumed we were upset about being taken out of the game, and they were right. That was enough for them.

When practice was scheduled to start that afternoon, our coach announced that the two of us had something to say to the team. We apologized. Later, one of my other friends and teammates said she knew we weren't sorry and she didn't care that we weren't. She thought it was dumb that we were made to apologize. She was glad we decided to stay on the team.

Looking back at that experience, I would feel sad for the two girls who just wanted a chance to play ball. They were only kids. The anger that rose into my chest would surprise me with its force. I am older and have a better understanding of what it means to be a woman in the world. I know what it is to be shamed. I know the burden of carrying shame like a disease in my body. I have fallen into my place in a culture where women are expected to play small—to literally shrink their bodies as much as possible—and have their voices silenced.

My coach, an adult I adored and respected, had failed me. He had taken away my power by shaming me in front of my team. He and the athletic director humiliated me and offered no opportunity for me to learn from what I did. They didn't empower me with knowledge or better decision-making skills—or even basketball skills for that matter. My friend and I tried to stand up for ourselves in the only way we knew: to literally stand up for ourselves. We were still children, and we did what we thought we had to do to take a stand for ourselves.

It might have begun there. It was a power struggle larger than any I had encountered with my parents. I felt ashamed and powerless. Similar experiences followed. There were a few teachers who tried to shame me in front of my classmates. There was the boy I had known since fourth grade who refused to hear my "no" one night in the woods. It was the summer before I left for college. We were drunk in a park with our friends. He knocked me down. He forced himself onto me and into me. I blamed myself. I was mortified. I never told my parents. There were other boys after that one.

The more threatened I felt by people or circumstances, the quicker I would shrink into the shadows. Rather than facing rejection or confrontation or disappointing someone (my worst possible nightmare), I became as small and silent as humanly possible for a woman who is five foot ten. I didn't want to take up any space. I drank lots of beer to help me disappear. As I withdrew into myself, life felt harsher and more confusing. I wasn't sure how to navigate any of the trickier paths I crossed, and I often felt desperate and alone.

Eventually, there were no more power struggles. Before anyone could take it from me, I handed my power over. I relied on others for validation. My life was a game of solitaire, and I kept stacking the deck against myself. I blamed my losses on the Devil like my grandma had when she played cards.

Eventually, everyone I met was involved in a high-level conspiracy to bring me down: the guy who cut me off on the highway, the woman who didn't smile back at me at Target, the mom who didn't make eye contact with me in the pick-up line at school, and the doctor who talked over me when I tried to describe my symptoms. I was living my life from a place of powerlessness, and I didn't even know it. I thought that was the way I was supposed to live. I was at the mercy of others' desires, needs, and opinions. I thought I was supposed to parent at the mercy of my children. I thought it was the way I was supposed to show up for my mom as her daughter when my dad died—at the mercy of her needs.

After my dad died, I began to notice that I had no patience for anyone who appeared to be living purely for the sake of others—the martyrs and the victims. When met with any indication that a person was blaming someone or something else for personal troubles or sacrificing individual needs to meet the needs of someone else, I felt my blood pressure spike and heat rising into my chest. I became infuriated.

When I returned from my trip to Sedona, I began working with a life coach. I told Ken a story about a person who was really bothering me, and he said something that changed my life. He said, "You spot it, you got it."

Huh?

In the simplest terms, we mirror each other. Therefore, what I notice in others is a reflection of something that exists in me too.

Consequently, when someone I knew was blaming someone or something else for his or her troubles, I felt the heat rising in my chest. My reaction had very little to do with that person and everything to do with what she was mirroring back to me. I saw her as a victim because I was living my life as a victim. Her perceived lack of power in her own life infuriated me because I wasn't standing in my power.

For years, I had been living at the mercy of everyone and everything around me, and that way of living was no longer working for me. It was making me crazy. Living my life that way didn't align with the effort I was making to remain true to my feelings as I made my way with Grief. As I was allowing myself to feel and be honest about my feelings for the first time, I could no longer approach life at the mercy of it, my family, and all that we were experiencing. I could no longer play the role of a victim. In order to play a new role, I would have to take responsibility for my feelings instead of continuing to blame my feelings on others.

What followed was an excruciating journey toward the freedom that comes from owning one's power and place in the world. At first, I struggled to decipher where I ended and where others began (boundaries). This is still a challenge in my relationships with my family as my default, both as a woman and as a mother, is to take on what isn't really mine to carry (emotions, tasks, and even outcomes).

I suppose it always will be a challenge to back off from trying to carry my children's burdens, especially when it seems like life would be so much easier if I could just jump in and fix things for the people I love—or fix the whole world for that matter. I am learning to honor that all of us are on our own journeys. Along the way, it is up to us to own our mistakes and celebrate our victories. I can't do that for another person, and I sure as hell can't expect another person to do that for me.

Just as I chose to forgive my parents for the secrets they kept, I had to let them off the hook for doing the best they could with the (limited) resources they had. They were practically children themselves when they had me. Of course they were going to make some mistakes and, of course, as a grown woman, I can pick up the violin at any time and start playing it. Nobody is stopping me.

As I continue to face my insecurities, challenge my judgment, and conquer my impulsivities, I am learning to own the possibility that I can decide how to alter a situation. My ability to change course is not entirely dependent upon someone or something outside of me. I am unlearning the habits I developed in response to situations where I had given my power over to another person. Rather than staying silent, I am learning to speak up. Instead of hiding, I am learning to stand tall. I can stand my ground. Ultimately, I am learning that there is another way to live, and it is very different from the way I had been living. One of the biggest shifts in adapting to this new way of living is that as I forgive my parents and take back the power I once gave away, I am also forgiving myself for the mistakes I have made. Forgiving myself and letting myself off the hook are by far the most generous gifts I have given myself in this process.

As I dive into the practice of examining my responses to my interactions with others, I am developing more compassion for them as humans facing their own struggles. They are doing the best they can with what they have. Compassion is taking over the space previously occupied by the irritation, frustration, and self-doubt I felt when I thought another person had mistreated me.

I developed more compassion for myself. That compassion was essential as I allowed myself to truly experience and feel the emotions that arose in my grief. Judgment and shame were replaced by self-compassion. My hard edges continue to soften as I accept that I am a human facing my own struggles. I am doing the best I can with the resources I have. The self-doubt I carried for years opens the way for more self-confidence. While I am still learning the value of not taking things so personally, I've stopped assuming everyone in the world is out to get me when things get hard. As I release others from the expectations I set for them, I release the unrealistic expectations I have for myself. Compassion is a never-ending stew of soft, gentle ways of nourishing others and myself.

Digging deep into my past has helped me to understand the choices I've made along the way. No one has ever asked me to exist at their mercy—that was a choice I made for myself. I realized how I came to that choice, and I can take responsibility for how I move forward from here. When I saw myself as a victim of circumstance, I could never be satisfied. I was always left wanting. From this new perspective, I know I can propel myself up and out when I feel like I'm trapped underwater. I am only at the mercy of myself.

Seeking

I remember the police officer suggesting we might want a priest to visit us the night my dad died—or at least offering that as a possibility. I wonder if anything would have been different if a priest had come to us. Would my mom and Sarah and I had felt more peace when we woke the next morning in my mom's bed? Would we have known sooner that what we remembered as we woke wasn't really a bad dream but our new reality? Would we find comfort in knowing our beloved dad and husband was in heaven? Would we feel confident in our belief that there even is a place like heaven?

Grief raises many questions. I understood that most of my questions could not be answered with any real accuracy, but I didn't stop asking. I didn't stop wondering. In fact, from the moment I first encountered God, heard about heaven, or feared hell, I never stopped wondering whether any of it was real. I never stopped wondering if I could really trust it. I never stopped wondering if I could ever really have that thing called faith. The question that troubled me most was whether I was even eligible to receive God's love.

I have probably been "saved" more than any other sinner on earth. The first time I was saved I was at Vacation Bible School at a First Baptist Church in my hometown. I was about seven years old. One of the moms in my neighborhood taught at the Vacation Bible School, and each morning, she packed her station wagon with her own kids and kids from our neighborhood and took us to Vacation Bible School. We went every day for a week. I listened closely to the lessons and bit my lip as I concentrated on making crafts. I fumbled over the words of Bible verses as my cohorts recited them in singsong.

I was saved on the altar at that Baptist church for several consecutive summers. I raised my hand, I left my seat, and I kneeled before Jesus. I waited for the release I felt each time I was saved. I was fascinated by the idea of Jesus dying on the cross for my sins. I didn't quite understand sins, but they sounded bad. I was comforted by the image of Jesus forgiving me for mine. I felt a sense of peace and relief pass over me each, and every time I was saved, I felt covered. What could be better than that? *I am saved.* What I relished most though was the blissful feeling I experienced as part of a giggly community of sweaty little bodies crammed together in a church pew singing "Jesus Loves Me." I belonged. I was connected. I was loved.

Around the time I was in third grade, my dad's truck broke down in front of the home of a kind, elderly couple named Don and Ethelyn. Don was a shorter, wispy white-haired man who wore eyeglasses. When he looked at me, his expression was mischievous—like he was about to get us into trouble. Ethelyn towered over him and was beautifully poised. She was an elegant woman who only wore skirts with her nude-colored nylons and black high heels. She had the most beautiful white hair rolled into huge curls and tucked into fancy hats. They invited us to attend Hallers Corners Free Methodist Church one Sunday, and my parents heartily accepted their thoughtful invitation.

The church was housed in a tiny old white building on the corner of two roads. The land where it stands still looks exactly the same as it did back then. There is a sprawling farm on one side of the church and a parsonage on the other. Across the street is an empty field. Only the sign on the church is different.

As seems to be the case for most churches, there were some young families, families with older children, and some senior citizens in the congregation. As the pastor prayed, one of the elders quietly chanted, "Yes, Jesus." I always wondered if I should chime in. I didn't. They counted Bibles and visitors each Sunday. The ritual of the service—the praying and the hymn singing and the Bible counting—was comforting in its simplicity and predictability.

My dad frequently brought his guitar to church with us. He played it and sang hymns as a solo act and with the congregation. My sister would walk up to the front of the church while he was singing and hang on his pant leg. The first time I ever remember hearing "Amazing Grace" was when my dad sang it at church. I thought it was the most beautiful song I had ever heard, and I fell into a trance when I heard my dad singing it.

Each time I heard him sing, I thought, *My dad is not a wretch*! My mom exchanged potluck dish recipes with the women of the congregation. I was delighted when she started making her own "pretzel salad." It was a scrumptious combination of toasted pretzels, a cream cheese mixture, and cherry-pie filling. There may have been some Cool Whip involved. We were fairly active in the congregation and attended church there for years. Being part of the church community, I felt like I had a place somewhere just as I had in Vacation Bible School. I felt connected.

When Dan and I settled into our second home, we began a tradition of hosting Thanksgiving dinner there. My dad began his own tradition of playing his guitar and singing "Amazing Grace" before dinner. I treasure the few moments I had each year when I stopped obsessing over the dinner details and looked up to take in the scene before me: a long row of tables pushed together, lovingly set with cloths, dishes, and fresh flowers. In front of each place setting stood a person I adored: Dan, our children, my parents, my sister and her husband, my in-laws, my sister's in-laws, and anyone else who needed a place to give thanks that day.

With such tenderness and fierceness too, a balance that my dad struck so well, he played his guitar and sang the most beautiful hymn ever written. I was moved to the core. We have no known recording of him singing "Amazing Grace," but I have a picture of him singing at the head of the table from the Thanksgiving before he died. I cherish it. I also treasure the feeling that comes in moments of shared experience: a shared song, a shared conversation, or a shared love. I've been chasing that feeling my entire life. While that feeling is in large part about a sense of belonging and community to me, it is also in appreciation of a connection to something bigger that we all share.

The experiences I had in church made early imprints on my long and winding spiritual path. My mom was raised Catholic, and my dad was Episcopalian. I think, as part of an ongoing effort to reject convention, they chose to raise their children in neither of their churches. Even as a very young child—and even when I didn't attend church with my parents—a spiritual connection was present in my life and in our home.

I followed my parents on hikes through woods and fields. We swam in lakes and gazed at star-filled skies. All the while, I felt what I now know as God's presence. I remember feeling an enormous sense of community when we went canoeing with a social-activist group called Spark. I was just a kid, but I knew in my bones that we were part of something bigger.

Nature was our church, and anyone was welcome to join our congregation. As I grew up and heard my friends' stories about going to church and heard about my cousins taking their First Communions, I feared we were doing it all wrong in my family. When I attended church services with friends and family, I stumbled awkwardly through them. I had heard that God speaks to us in the voice He knows we will hear. When I was in church, I was too confused and afraid of looking dumb to listen for God's voice. I rarely heard it there.

I spent much of my adolescence and young adulthood confusing church with God. I didn't understand that I was already a spiritual being or that I already had a relationship with God. I didn't understand that it just looked different than the one my friends had. God was always speaking to me in the voice I would hear. He spoke to me in the wind, in the songs the birds sang, and in the waves that crashed against the shore. I didn't know what I heard was God's voice.

When I thought about God speaking to me, I imagined a deep, booming voice I would hear clearly. I would be sure when I heard it. I might have been waiting for a formal invitation from God to listen. I wanted there to be a single being—one body of God—that covered all of us.

I was bothered by the ways organized religion caused so much angst in the world. With so many wide and varying beliefs, no one body could be the right match for everyone. And if it could be, that would make a huge part of the population wrong in what they believed. When it didn't seem like God could work for everyone, I found it harder to establish my own relationship with God. I began to doubt whether I even believed in God. Eventually, I gave up trying to know God.

And then my first child was born.

As I held James for the first time outside my body and he nursed contentedly at my breast, I knew with all my heart and soul and in every corner of my mind and body that there had to be something bigger. The only thing I could think of that was ever said to be that big and bold and beautiful was God. James made me a believer. In those first few moments of motherhood, I was completely taken aback by the sheer enormity of the absolute miracle of creating life, growing that life inside my very own body, and giving birth to that life. That life immediately came to be known as my child.

Baby James was so perfect, so angelic, so pure, and so real. I couldn't imagine ever again questioning God's existence. With the birth of James, I was welcomed into a community more expansive than any I had ever experienced: motherhood. I was instantly connected to all the mothers past, present, and future. Only God could oversee that kind of community. I could see then how that breadth of oversight could not possibly be limited to the confines of a building or even one singular belief system. I didn't have to hear a thing to know God was real.

And then my dad died.

In the days after my dad's death, it seemed that the people I knew to be people of faith had a leg up in the grief department. They seemed so sure of the fate of their beloveds who had passed on before them. They seemed secure in that blanket of faith: as God's children, by the grace of God, in grief and in mourning. They seemed so sure that their loved ones were in a better place. *What place, for the love of God, could be better than right here?* They seemed sure that their loved ones had crossed through the Pearly Gates to a magnificent place called heaven. And they knew that someday they would be reunited with their loved ones in heaven. I had God, but I didn't have heaven. It wasn't easy for me to accept the existence of heaven or find comfort in my dad landing there. I refused to believe in hell or Satan.

I refused to believe that the death of a loved one was ever God's plan (as some people I knew had suggested).

Despite my conviction that my dad's death was not part of any plan, I envied the people who said those words with such ease. I had heard the words many times, most painfully after I miscarried what would have been our second child. I determined that it was much easier to have faith in a plan when everything in your life seemed to be going according to that plan.

At the time of my miscarriage, I believed that for me, for my family, and for Dan and me, there didn't seem to be a very good plan. But then, right before my dad's death, things had begun to fall into place. I would even say my life seemed perfect. I knew we were blessed, and I was incredibly grateful for that.

I didn't know much about being faithful in a religious sense, but I felt sure that God was looking over me. I prayed and gave thanks, and I thought God and I had a pretty good thing going. Up until my dad's death, my beliefs were working out for me. In the face of grief, I desperately wished I had more to fall back on.

In the days after my dad's death, even buoyed by the love that surrounded me, I again began to even question whether I really believed in God. My dad, forever the seeker, told me not too long before he died that if he had to say, he would say he was a Buddhist. Buddhist thought spoke to me, but it was not calling me to pursue the path to Buddhism. I didn't even know if I could purse that path. I began to think that maybe, instead of one set of beliefs being right and all the others wrong, that maybe they were all right. Maybe there is one God that speaks to us in the voice He knows we will hear and maybe that voice manifests in different ways for each of us. Maybe when we die, we end up wherever we imagine we are going to end up: heaven, a hole in the ground, stuck in spirit form roaming the streets at night. It drove me crazy that I didn't know.

So, instead of putting my faith in God when my dad died, I had faith in nothing. I even lost faith in myself. All of life seemed chaotic and coincidental. Everything I knew to be true was called to question. There was no reason for anything. And I was alone. I again longed for something that told me what to believe, and even more than that, I longed for the confidence that came with that belief. I wanted to be able to stand up and say, "It's all going to be okay." A small part of me still thought there had to be something bigger than me at play, but I didn't know what to call it. I wasn't sure what form it took, and I was too sad and too tired to try to figure it out.

As I studied grief, I inevitably ventured into the subject of life after death. It was in the words of the books I read that I first heard Spirit speaking to me directly. I softened. I opened. I began to again see that there is indeed something bigger than me, and it did go by many names: Allah, Buddha, and God. And it went by names like She, He, Creator, Goddess, the Divine Mother, Spirit, and the Universe. I knew that what those names really stood for was something very big indeed; they stood for love. They stood for a big, all-encompassing, universal love. I was confident that an even greater God than any of us could ever imagine existed. A love God. Anything I read or heard or inquired about then led back to love.

It became clear to me that God has always spoken to us in the very same language: love. We translate that language for ourselves. We interpret it in many ways. We interpret that language for ourselves or follow other people's interpretations. To experience God's love, we must be able to do it within the constructs that make sense to us. God's love is truly incomprehensible to us. We cannot even fathom what it means to be loved by God. We have only an inkling of an understanding of what it means to be loved like that, and that inkling is enough! The specifics of our beliefs mean little in comparison to our ability to keep piecing our lives together with the one common thread: universal love.

Immediately following my dad's death, I mistakenly came to wonder if I had somehow failed in developing a good enough relationship with God. It didn't seem like God was there for me. I wasn't clear or confident enough in my beliefs to let them sustain me or to allow myself to be comforted by God's love.

I didn't trust that it was there for me. I mistakenly thought that if I had done it all differently, I would have been at peace with my dad's death. I began to think that I wasn't truly worthy of God's love. It seemed that God's love was something very special that I couldn't access. I now know that no matter how crooked or broken a path a person takes—and no matter what ways a person practices to deepen his or her relationship with God—God's love is accessible and always there for all of us.

For as long as I can remember, I have related to angels. I felt the presence of angels when I was a child. When I saw figurines or art featuring angels, I felt a kindred connection to them. As I opened to the possibility of God in the months after my dad passed away, I began to recognize an angelic presence in my life again. I read books about angels. I practiced writing to my angels and receiving their messages. I appreciated how angels acted as messengers of God, giving me signs that God and love were all around me. I recalled how angels spoke to me throughout my life on behalf of God. It was so refreshing to be reacquainted with my angels; they were like old friends. I could see them celebrating our reunion. While we were in Sedona, my angels spoke up a great deal.

In Sedona, I met some of my other spirit guides and became reacquainted with some of my ancestors. After so many years of trying desperately to understand what it meant to be loved by God, I gave in to the love that surrounded me. I let it wrap its arms around me. I no longer felt the need to understand any of the messengers or guides or beings. I knew that I was never meant to understand.

The more I opened to the possibilities that there was love all around me (and that there were helpers everywhere), the more I could see the acts of angels in my everyday life. I learned that while the angels are always with us and watch over us, they tend not to intervene in day-to-day functions until we ask for help. I learned that I could keep writing to them and even speak to them directly, and they would answer. I now ask my angels for all kinds of help—for help with everything from easing the pain of my aching heart to clearing traffic so I can make a safe turn. They always answer—although not always in the ways I want them to answer. They are eager to help. I love to imagine them waiting in the wings to shed light, to help us with healing and growth, and to show us miracles and grace. I am grateful for their presence.

I love how my angels conspire with other messengers. Months after my dad died, one of my dear friends lost her dad. I was dreading having to attend his visitation because I honestly didn't think I could handle the emotions that might arise. I thought my own grief might be triggered at the visitation, and I knew it would be difficult to see my friend grieving the loss of her beloved father. I really wanted to be fully present for her, but I couldn't imagine how that was possible. I asked my angels to carry me.

On the way to the funeral home, I passed a deer on the side of the road. It was as if she had been waiting for me to pass. She was staring right at me. I nodded and smiled, knowing that deer have also been with me since I was a little girl. I once went "hunting" with my dad. We dressed in camouflage, painted our faces, and watched in awe as the deer went about their business around us. No animals were harmed on our "hunting trip."

I drove the rest of the way to the visitation, and I didn't break down. I was present for my friend. I hugged her mother. I met other members of her family. On my way home, the deer was on the other side of the road. She was standing in the brush again: staring, waiting, watching, and guiding me home. I find a world of comfort in knowing that animals guide, protect, teach, and serve as beacons of hope, wisdom, love, and courage.

Angels and messengers try all kinds of tricks to remind us that we are loved and not alone. They use numbers, music, special songs, feathers, pennies, heart-shaped rocks, rainbows, and birds. They are tireless in their efforts to show us that we are surrounded in love. This love thing is big. It is huge. It cannot be contained in any one belief or practice. Even a person who already feels completely loved and cherished is only experiencing a tiny bit of what it possible. It is that big, and it really is for everybody.

We are connected to one another by God's love. We are one. It is the ultimate community. We show up for each other as the face of God. When we hear just the words we needed to hear from a friend or a stranger, that is God talking. That is God's love revealing itself to us. What if we could all trust that we are literally woven and bound together by the very same love? One of the biggest fallacies in grief (and even in life) is that we are alone in our suffering. We are not alone. As the saying goes, we are spiritual beings having a human experience. Beliefs are beliefs. Grief is grief. Suffering is suffering. Mistakes are mistakes. Flaws are flaws. Beliefs, grief, suffering, mistakes, and flaws are all part of being human.

In our culture, we use our human qualities to separate ourselves from each other and alienate groups from one another. In truth, these human qualities are part of the human experience and bind us together. We are loved—no matter what we believe, no matter how much we do or don't suffer, no matter who or what we grieve, no matter how long it takes, no matter how many mistakes we make, no matter how many times we change our minds or fall off our wagons, and no matter how flawed we are—just because we are human. Maybe spirituality simply refers to the ways we navigate our humanity as spiritual beings. Spirituality can be so many things. It can be whatever we need it to be to make this human journey more peaceful for ourselves and for others.

Being loved is part of the contract we make with the universe before we are born.

We say, "Yes, I'll be human."

The universe says, "Good, and I will love you and support you without judgment. You can access me anywhere." Some say that in the course of making that contract, we get to choose which lessons we will learn when we come to earth as humans. We choose those we will travel with. We choose our adversities and the ways we will make our exits.

I often think about the contracts we may have made as souls. I think about my dad slipping away while reading in his shed—alone—and the loss I experience each time I play out alternative scenarios in my mind. In the most desirable scene, we know the end is near, we say a proper good-bye, and we gather around his bedside to keep him company while he draws his last breath.

The idea that my dad's sweet soul may have had a say or a choice in his death before he even grew feet on earth comforts me when I wrestle with what was and was not.

I wonder why this and not that. My dad suffered a great deal through his life. While it may still take years before I can fully accept that there was no knowing—and no last good-bye—I am grateful for my dad's swift death. He experienced no additional suffering. He may have felt some brief discomfort, but there was no pain. Ultimately, above all else, I am at peace with this new and different kind of knowing. No matter how he died, I know he was ushered out of this life surrounded by the very same force of love that led him into it. I find peace in the fact that we are supported in life and death by an unimaginable force of universal love.

Nothing has the power to intervene on God's behalf because we walk with spirit ourselves. We hold hands, and—in all ways—we actually are spirit. God guides us toward tools He knows will resonate with us (the voices we need to hear), and He loves us with no conditions. For some people, the tools that resonate are a church and a Bible. For me, it is Lake Michigan and the sky, the water, and the stones I find there. It is the rock on the beach where I first spoke with my dad as a spirit. It is in my very own backyard.

As I deepen my own spiritual practices and relationship with God, I care less about how what I do compares to what others do. I am becoming more intimate with God. As is the case in any close relationship, the more intimate we become, the further we move from caring about other people's opinions or perceptions of our relationship.

The seeking, the questioning, and the wondering are important components of my spiritual journey. I will continue to be curious about the ways people worship God, honor creation, move through the seasons, and celebrate rites of passage. The difference now is that I know none of us are more or less worthy in the eyes of God. None of us are more or less lovable. I am secure in that knowing, and I marvel at the possibilities for our planet if we all opened to receiving God's love. What if we trusted in the abundance of that universal love so much that we loved each other automatically, freely, and without conditions? What if our interpretations of the language of that love could somehow merge into one understanding that love is really and truly all there is?

Among the people I know who seem grounded in faith, no matter how they practice spirituality, they are committed to learning and growing in faith and in their relationships with God. They are committed to their practices. They practice both inside and outside of churches. They may inherit practices or develop their own practices, but those practices always honor and celebrate God, life, and all of creation. These practices are rooted in love—in dipping into that deep, wide, unimaginable, never-ending, and all-encompassing pool of God's love.

I no longer wonder what happened to my dad after he died. His spirit is with me and in many other places at once. He is now a spiritual being having a spirit experience. I cannot even begin to imagine what that is like, and I don't need to know. I cannot even fathom how huge or deep or wide the universe is, and that is okay. I am at peace with the mystery of all that is. I know all of it is made in, bound with, and sustained by love. I trust in that love. I trust that the practices I have developed to honor, to appreciate, and to ask for guidance from God are pure.

I am respectfully and profoundly grateful for all the religions and spiritual practices I've encountered along my path. By way of these experiences, I have been able to establish my own practices. I can better appreciate how important it is for other people to have similar experiences and choose what works best for them. Perhaps my relationship to God mirrors my relationship to myself—and to others.

The more I accept and receive God's love and the more I turn inward for approval instead of looking for approval outside myself, the more space I have in my heart to accept and love myself. I also have more space in my heart to accept and love others.

Making

My mom called to tell me my dad's old truck was totaled. It was almost like hearing my dad died all over again. The truck was the last operating piece of him.

Sarah started driving my dad's truck after he died. Her husband was driving it when it was totaled. Only by the grace of God was Nate virtually unharmed in the accident. Thank you, God (and thank you, Dad). The truck still smelled like my dad. Before Nate's accident, when I saw the truck in my sister's driveway, I liked to pretend my dad was inside the house. He spent so much time in that truck. It was an extension of him. I found comfort in knowing it was out there, still moving, still alive, still breathing in the way a truck breathes. I was surprised to be so moved by the truck's demise, yet it made sense to me that I would have liked it to stay around to forever remind me of my dad.

My mom and I drove to the junkyard to see the truck. I took some metal cutters with me, thinking I could use some metal from the truck in a collage. I even thought about making jewelry out of it. Cutting through the metal hurt my hand so I only ended up with some small pieces, some shattered glass, and a plastic piece from the side of the truck that said "Ranger."

My collection of truck remains sat in the same place for over a year. I finally began my project on the fifth anniversary of my dad's death. It is interesting how anniversaries work. No matter how good I feel as the anniversary approaches—how sane, how content, how at peace—the days leading up to the actual anniversary knock me on my ass. The cells in my body remember the trauma of the night my dad died, and even though I feel mentally and emotionally fine, my body, mind, and spirit feel stress. My body reminds the rest of me what happened. It rallies its counterparts and invites Grief to come out to play. Making a piece of art in my dad's memory seemed like a peaceful way to spend the fifth anniversary of my dad's death. I thought I might even be able to reprogram my cells with new memories. I thought if I gave my body space that day, the force of its memories might not be so disabling.

I started with an art board and painted it with a black onyx background. I added shades of Payne's gray and blended some of it into the black paint with titanium white. I ripped into photocopies of my dad's handwritten song lyrics, selecting the stanzas that spoke loudest to me:

> She's such a beautiful woman
> She has a beauty that's beyond compare (2x)
> When you look upon her beauty …
> We had two beautiful daughters and our
> grandchildren number four

We love having them, and we'd love to have
some more!
Ain't it beautiful?
Her beauty is such a wonderful thing.
It brought the world more beauty.
It makes my heart sing!

I wondered what word my dad would have used to rhyme with five if he had lived long enough to meet his fifth grandchild. Would he edit the lyrics? Write a new song? I ripped and glued the pieces of paper down with collage medium. It was like sifting through all the stories that comprised my life, discarding what no longer worked for me, and using what was left to create something new.

I added a photo of my dad performing at a gig and a copy of a sketch he had done of a man's face in the margin of his lyrics. A self-portrait? I secured the pieces of his truck and broken glass onto my creation with E-6000. I played music. I lit candles. I watched in wonder as the flame danced with a breeze that came in through the window. I felt my dad's presence. I felt peace.

With each object I added, the hurt rising in my heart subsided. I reclaimed choice in the matter of my dad's death. Even though I had no power to make choices about his death or the ways we could and could not say good-bye when he passed, I could choose how to craft a new story. It was a story of remembering, of cherishing, and of honoring these pieces of my dad's life—and mine. The creative process is where my most powerful healing occurs.

Part of my quest to grieve properly entailed giving myself space to sit with all my stories: the characters, the narratives, the beginnings, and the endings. *How do I reconcile the stories?* The answer came in the form of making art. My mom and I took an online art class through the Brave Girls Club, and that opened the floodgates to an entire thriving community of artists, writers, and teachers. I thought I had died and gone to heaven.

I had always gotten lost in creating when I was a little girl. Even my mud pies were carefully crafted masterpieces. After adding just the right amount of water to my dirt, I loved sinking my hands into my concoctions. I loved the feeling of mixing the dirt with the water and patting the pie into place. I decorated the tops of my pies with rocks. Although I didn't know it at the time, it was never about the mud pie. Instead, my experience was all about the creative process—making something that never before existed in that way, in that shape, or at that time.

When I was eleven, I started my first journal. Writing has since helped me process what is happening in my life. When I write, my soul speaks to me. In the early years of motherhood, I rarely made time to write in my journal. I have a small stack of journals from those years that I started but never finished. In that space freed by grief after my dad's death, I rediscovered writing and making art, two practices I had enjoyed sporadically as an adult but had mostly neglected. Reconnecting with those practices was like coming home to myself after a long journey to a faraway place.

Each of us is born a creative being, and we honor that through the act of creating. We honor our Creator, and we honor all that has ever been created. Creating connects us to our own hearts and to the hearts of others. Creating is essential. Sharing what we create can help us thrive in unimaginable ways. Keeping some of our creations to ourselves can also offer a unique kind of magic.

What I have come to appreciate most about my dad since his passing is that no matter what was happening around him, he remained true to his heart and his art by following its calling to play the blues. When I was a little girl and my dad played his guitar at family gatherings, I would sometimes become embarrassed. I rolled my eyes when he pulled out his guitar. I quickly assessed the expressions of faces around the room, looking for validation that playing his music would be okay. I wished he could be more like my friends' dads. I thought my life would be so much easier if I could just buy him a tie for Father's Day. My dad wore plaid, flannel work shirts and old T-shirts. None of the Hallmark cards I found in the store fit his personality. He didn't fish. He didn't watch football. He didn't golf or wear ties to work. He played the guitar, he smoked pot, and he read science fiction. He was really smart about politics. He was an amateur actor and an activist. He listened to NPR in the car. He ate apple cores and made fried peanut butter sandwiches. When I was a little girl, he put my hair in a ponytail—and he put his own hair in a ponytail too.

In as much as I thought I wanted a dad like all the others, my free-spirited, non-conforming dad captivated me. Being his daughter was a very special experience for me. When he pulled his guitar out to play in front of family, I believe I knew how much my dad's music meant to him—and I wanted it to mean something to the people with whom he shared it. I'm not sure he ever cared much about that because when and what he played came straight from his heart and soul. His soul spoke in music.

I cannot think of a single time I saw him play that everybody didn't seem to be enjoying his music. He was a gifted musician and performer. My dad shined when he was on a stage. He expanded in the exchange of energy that happened between him and the people for whom he played. My dad inspired people with his music. He inspired me. Rediscovering my passion for creating brought me closer to my dad.

I tried many different creative practices after my dad died. I enjoyed making collages in art journals because it combined all the crafty endeavors I ever enjoyed—mainly writing and scrapbooking. My mom and I took a class in Zentangle, which is a method that uses repeating patterns to make abstract art. It is done on a small square tile of 100 percent cotton paper with black ink. Each of the patterns has a name—some are "official" Zentangle patterns, and some are patterns created by those who teach and practice Zentangle. The process of Zentangle is a moving meditation. I clearly remember sitting in that first class and feeling the calming effects of making marks on my tile. It was remarkable how something so simple could so quickly mesmerize a group of students. Except for the flute music playing in the background, the room was silent. A roomful of chatty women was silent. I hadn't experienced anything like that since college exams.

When our instructor told us about her experience becoming a Certified Zentangle Teacher (CZT), I quickly felt the benefits of the process. *I could do this! I want to do this! I want to share this with people!* As I learned more of the Zentangle patterns, I began to see patterns in everything. For me, part of the beauty of a Zentangle practice is the ability to see how we are all connected by the patterns made from the symbols that occur in our lives. Many of them are age-old universal symbols like circles, spirals, crosses, and crescent moons that instantly connect us to the marks made throughout history. They are the symbols used in hieroglyphics, geometry, and other patterns we use today. The patterns evoke emotions and serve as signs for the roads we've traveled and the roads that lie before us. Zentangle, which is often described as a simple way of making abstract art, was so much more than an art form to me. It was a way to connect to myself, to others, and to billions of years of history. During that first class, I decided I wanted to become a CZT—and my mom did too.

When my mom and I arrived at the hotel for our CZT training, I was so nervous. It had been so long since I had done any kind of "business" travel, and the thought of having to enter a huge room filled with strangers was intimidating. It occurred to me that these strangers might actually see my art or watch as I made art, and that scared me too. I knew it would take every last bit of courage I had to share my own art—and myself—with other people.

What transpired was a beautiful few days with some of the loveliest, most creative, and most passionate people I have ever met. The Zentangle founders (Rick Roberts and Maria Thomas) were delightful. They shared stories about their lives like we were all old friends.

I was amazed when the large conference room fell silent as we all put pencil to paper to begin our Zentangle creations together. Creating and connecting with others through art felt like coming home to me. Despite my fears and insecurities about sharing my art with others, I came away wildly inspired to share Zentangle.

I often hear people say they are not creative; they don't even try art or creative writing. In my heart, I know we are all creative beings. I know we were meant to create as we were created. I loved that Zentangle was accessible to a broad range of people. It is something anyone can do, and it still carries all the healing powers that other forms of art carry. It allows us to slow down, go within, and connect. It allowed me to externalize my pain and deal with whatever remained unresolved inside me in a very concrete, hands-on way. The marks and symbols expressed things I could not express with words. As I considered sharing something so powerful with others, I felt like I was growing wings and preparing to fly. I think in many ways, I was coming alive.

Howard Thurman is often quoted for having said, "Don't ask yourself what the world needs. Ask yourself what makes you come alive and then go do that. Because what the world needs is people who have come alive."

When I am writing, painting, making collages, or practicing Zentangle, I feel more alive than I do ordinarily. If there is one thing I want for my children, it is for them to figure out what makes them come alive. It is such a disservice to oneself to keep from doing what makes you feel most alive. It is essential to your being that you let yourself come alive.

I think we are fundamentally obligated to tune into our hearts and their longings and follow the guidance we are given. We know—and have always known—what matters to us most, but we forget sometimes. It isn't likely that I will ever be found on a stage playing a guitar and singing the blues (at least not in public), but I think I can better relate to what my dad experienced as a performer now that I am developing my own practice of sharing my work with the world. It makes me so happy to know that my dad stayed true to his art until the day he died. I imagine he continues to stay true to it in the afterlife as well.

For me, the act of piecing things together—papers, paints, collages, words, ideas, or universal signs and symbols—is like making maps to my heart and soul. As I literally sift through all these parts and assemble them into something new, I figuratively piece myself back together. This process helps me remember what matters most to me. I cannot claim to tell anyone how to navigate grief because part of the process of grieving is figuring out how to make it through for yourself. However, I know from my own experiences and from hearing what works for others, that the process of making or creating is incredibly healing.

With writing and with images, with gardens and meals, with sculpture and carving, with sewing and stitching, with breaking down and assembling, in composing and playing, in upcycling and in repurposing, in music and in dance, in all sorts of creative ways, we are able to express ourselves in ways we cannot through conversation. We can process feelings we may not even know we have. We can allow feelings and experiences—trauma—to rise and be released through our creative work. These practices allow our souls to speak to us, and they remind us what matters most.

My passion for practicing the creative process inspired me to take the broken remnants of my Dad's old truck and make art with them. I am grateful that my grief made space for my creativity. As much as I would not have expected this to be true, it is a reality that both grief and creativity give us opportunities to take our own broken pieces and breathe new life into them. Perhaps the creative process is all about making something new. Making something new is making something come alive. Creativity makes us come alive.

Reflecting

It has been five years since my dad died. He would have been sixty-eight years old today. I imagine that if he were still alive, he might be showing signs of aging by now. He still seemed like he would last forever when he passed. It's hard to imagine him moving at a slower pace. I can't imagine watching as his mental capacity diminished. I would hate to see him ill or suffering. I trust that it was his time to go when he left us. It was what was agreed upon in the sacred contract he made with the universe when he agreed to come to earth and give it a go as a human. And I wonder what it would be like if we hadn't lost him. It is strange to always be walking a line between acceptance and denial. Back and forth, I move forward with purpose and stumble with doubt. It is a two-step dance I have come to know so well, yet the back and forth of it never fails to surprise me.

James just turned thirteen, and I am sitting with the possibilities of what might have been if my dad were still alive. Would they celebrate this rite of passage into teendom with a camping trip? A jam session? Would I watch as they closed their eyes, nodded their heads, and tapped their toes to the beat in unison as they play their guitars? Together.

When a person dies, we are quick to point out to those who mourn that they will always have their memories. We point out that memories are something to cherish. I see that, and I am grateful for the many memories I have with my dad. I am even grateful for the bad memories. At the same time, as is always the case with grief, I sit with the reality that I am grateful for the memories I have and heartbroken by those we will never make with my dad.

James was seven when my dad died. Alexander was four, and Sophia was two. The other day, our nanny of four years told me she is moving to another state. Sophia was devastated. She burst into tears and yelled, "No! Why? I don't want her to leave!"

Tears formed in my eyes as I remembered James yelling something similar when we told him my dad had died: *No! Why? I didn't want him to die!*

"I know, honey," I said to Sophia. "It is so hard when someone you love leaves."

Selfishly maybe, I noticed that my daughter would never feel that kind of grief over the loss of my father, her Papaw.

While the memories I have with my dad are mostly comforting, none of us will make any new memories with him. James will not celebrate becoming a teenager with my dad. My dad will never welcome James or Alexander into manhood. Sophia might never miss him. For as long as my children are growing and reaching milestones in their lives, I will be keeping track of what my dad is missing. I will be keenly aware of his absence in the photos we take to commemorate these special occasions. I will wish for a hug from him and for his nod of approval. I anticipate a sense of loss with every gain we make in time and achievement.

Today, I enjoyed a cup of coffee and a slice of pecan pie because they were two of my dad's favorites. I wear a ponytail in my hair because his hair was in a ponytail when I last saw him. I add a plaid flannel shirt for good measure. I embody what he was and can no longer be. I miss him, and I feel his spirit.

Before my dad's death, I think I was partly motivated to find truth so I could follow it. I wanted to do the "right thing." After I lost my dad—and realized that I had been living on autopilot—I felt more lost than ever. I thought I was farther from the truth than I had ever been, and I imagined that if I hadn't been so lost, life after the loss of my dad would have made more sense to me. In my grief, I learned that my real quest in life is not in seeking the one thing that is true for all of us—the meaning of life—but rather in seeking what is true for me.

In the way he lived his life, my dad embodied the truths I was seeking. By the time he died, I was no longer paying attention. My dad was a subtle teacher. His lessons weren't forced upon me; honestly, I'm not sure it was ever his intention to teach me anything. He and my mom loved my sister and me unconditionally. In doing so, they showed us how to love a child. My dad pursued his passions without restrain or apology, and he encouraged others to do the same. He was devoted to lifelong learning and practicing his art: guitar, writing, woodworking, sketching, and life.

In all of his lyrics my mom finds scrawled on scrap paper and tucked into journals, I see how the magic happens in the process. My dad taught me that to have written or created or made something new is satisfying, but I have found that the biggest blessings come through the creative process. After my dad's death, I came to see that God and the universe and the love held within us are bigger than we can imagine.

Grief taught me how to be strong and gentle all at once. It taught me how to hold fear and hope with both hands. It taught me how to be angry and compassionate toward the same person at the same time. Grief (and life essentially) is where I can experience two conflicting emotions at one time. In my grief, I have felt excruciatingly vulnerable and amazingly brave.

When I look back at the way my dad shared his music and spoke out about the issues that mattered to him, I see that being vulnerable really does require a great deal of bravery. My dad always told me to stand up straight. He told me not to mumble when I spoke. It was his way of telling me that it was okay for me take up space and use my voice. I wasn't listening. He taught me the value of service to others, of community, of play, and of rest. He taught me how to advocate for my needs and desires by staying true to his—no matter the cost. He taught me to enjoy bacon and butter and coffee. He taught me to listen closely to NPR, to read other people's stories, and then to go on and write my own story.

My mom was gardening, cooking, and finding ways to help heal others as a teacher and a nurse. All through my life, my parents planted little seeds of wisdom in my soul.

They showed me that the beauty of life is not in what you accomplish or attain; it is in the process of living. I see that with great clarity now.

My path thus far has consisted of curves, bumps, and potholes. It has narrowed and widened, and I sometimes was required to walk without a path. I expect it will continue that way, and I know enough to welcome the pit stops since they hold so much potential for learning, for experiencing beauty, and for growth. The irony in my quest for truth is that the truth I sought was already present inside me. I came to this life with some of it, I absorbed the seeds dropped by my parents, and I went off on my own to find answers to life's great question. *What is the meaning of all this?*

Experiencing loss is a huge component of our lives. This is not entirely sad. It is allowing and accepting the reality we face when we lose something. In the physical sense, what is lost is no longer with us. No matter how much it mattered—and no matter how grateful we are for the space it once occupied in our lives—it is gone. We must go on without it. By allowing ourselves to experience loss again and again for as long as it takes, we can accept it.

When we deny ourselves the experience of loss or deny that it still hurts, we live in a state of unrest. When we allow ourselves to fully experience all of it, we find peace. It may be a constant process of hurting, allowing, and accepting. When we acknowledge the loss, we miss what we've lost, we hurt, we allow the hurt to surface, we sit with the pain and the gratitude we feel for having experienced anything that causes so much pain in its absence, and we accept it as a loss.

In this gracious space of acceptance, we know that loss is merely an experience. While we may be forever changed by the loss, it is not the death of us too. It is not the end.

I have learned to welcome loss as part of life. As I allow it to have its way with me, I trick myself into thinking that I am building immunity against devastation. I know it is merely a trick because I dread testing this theory. I also know that I am stronger than I might think in the face of loss. Loss presents itself in so many different forms. It is astonishing to think of the many things we risk losing in life: relationships, jobs, homes, visions, dreams, expectations, power, possessions, access to resources, body parts, confidence, contentment, joy, and pain. The list of potential losses goes on and on and on. Some of these things are traumatizing to lose, and some won't really be missed. Loss is constant. It is real. It is ongoing.

So many of us in live in fear of losing what matters to us. Some are even paralyzed by that fear. Entering any situation from a place of fear only invites more fear. If we knew that loss is inevitable and allowed ourselves to feel the full impact of loss when it occurs, we might not live in such fear. We might move through life with more ease.

Before losing my dad, I never thought about the extreme measures we take in society to save a life. It is remarkable what we will agree to in an effort to gain another week, month, or year of life. As much as we appear to value life in these situations, we are also afraid to live on a daily basis. We wait until we are in a crisis situation to take control of our lives. In our society we say we are "dying of (an illness)." We "fight" cancer and other diseases. We "struggle." We live in fear of death and loss.

Rather than identify as dying while alive, why not try to live out our final days the best we can? I have seen people try this. I am in awe of a person's capacity to live while dying. We can still allow ourselves to feel the impact of a disease and what it takes from us. Our struggle lies in resisting what is already there. The struggle doesn't change anything or take anything away. Allow what is there to be there. Accept it. Repeat. Let's gently disperse the energy we save for the bitter end bit by bit, like bees pollinating flowers, and play with the possibility that when we stop fighting against dying, we allow ourselves to fully experience living in rich and meaningful ways.

Our resistance to loss is partly responsible for the power it holds over us. Loss is painful, and it can derail us. There is no denying the devastation that follows loss, but when we fear loss and what it may bring with it, we suffer. This is not to say that accepting and allowing loss and its entourage will eliminate grieving. Instead, when we practice acceptance and allowance when we have the opportunity (which is always), we are not so afraid when faced with loss. Rather than resisting what we feel, we can allow ourselves to simply feel our feelings. By allowing ourselves to feel it all, we are less consumed by the fear of what we are feeling or what may follow. We really don't fear loss as much as we fear the impact it will have on us. Open to the impact. It may surprise you.

I think about the impact of loss a lot now. More of my friends are losing parents. More of my friends' parents are falling ill. Signs of my aunts and uncles' aging are becoming more apparent. Simultaneously, many of my friends and cousins are still caring for small children. Some of these children have experienced life-threatening illnesses. I've entered the stage of life where my friends and I are caught between two generations with big, ever-changing needs. We are now the "sandwich generation." It is heartbreaking on some days and infuriating on others. It can be difficult to wake up each morning knowing that someone's parent might be dying, someone else is being diagnosed, and children everywhere are battling depression and being bullied at school.

With loss, the only way out of despair is through. I want to move forward with trust. That is the only way I know to move through what lies ahead. It scares the shit out of me. *What could come from more loss? Am I up for that?* I can only hope that there will also be more beauty, more transformation, more grace, more ease, and more love. That would make quite an impact.

There are people who might be wondering why I'm not "over it" and thinking I should be. I will never be over losing my dad. I don't even want to be over it. My goal is not to be over it. My goal is to live with this loss like I would a new puppy. I will feed it when it is hungry and let it out when it is ready to be released. I will hold it and comfort it when it needs to be held, and I will play with it when it needs my attention.

Grief holds no power over me when I allow it to be what it is without judgment, without expectation, and without a timeline. Life holds a treasure trove of rich experiences for me to revel in when I live fully. Embracing my grief intensifies my joy. This is what works for me. This practice of allowing enriches my life in more ways than I can count. I am not afraid to remain open and to soften to this grief. I am not afraid to keep healing. I used to think I would one day be "healed," but now I see healing as something we do all the time. Some part of us is always healing. Some part of me will always need healing. I am healing and grieving losses all the time. Even when I hate grief, I can sit with this heartbreak for what was lost and gratitude for what it meant to me. I can sit with this loss and this life, this healing what is broken and sustaining what is whole, all of it all at once.

The most beautiful gift I receive in talking openly about grief is the privilege of being trusted to hold space for others' grief. I used to think that if we talked about loss more openly as a society and allowed ourselves to experience it more authentically, it might get easier. I no longer think that is true. What I do know is that the more we talk about grief and loss and the more we share our experiences with each other, the less alone we feel on our journeys through loss. That is why it is so important to share our stories about grief and loss—without qualifying the loss or trying to minimize the enormity of our feelings. Embracing loss together helps us see the ways in which we are connected to one another. While the experience of grief will be different for everyone, the need to grieve is the same. Nothing good comes from dismissing our feelings or our experiences around grief and trying to pretend we aren't hurting.

Saying it's going to be okay to those who mourn is fine because we know it will be okay eventually, but we need to allow them the space and time to first sit with it not being okay. Hearing "he is in a better place" or "it was his time" is not likely to be comforting. We need to be able to sit with a person in mourning in her darkest moments and say nothing. We must only listen. We can offer hugs, a box of tissues, and a warm cup of tea. When we have allowed time for her to completely empty out, we can say things like, "I am sorry this is happening. I will stay here with you."

No matter how hard it is to sit and watch as someone we care about suffers in grief, we must do this for each other. We must allow ourselves the opportunity to show up true for each other. That is the meaning of life: to show up, to make space, and to allow what needs to be heard or seen or felt to be heard, seen, and felt. We have to listen, act based on what we've heard, love, and be open to being loved.

As I sit with the treasures I've discovered in grief since the night my dad died, it is hard to imagine I am even the same person. I was so scared. I was shocked by my dad's unexpected death, terrified by my mom's sadness, and not at all confident I could move on. I still have days where I wonder how to keep going. They are just part of the process now. I wonder. I wait. And then, eventually, I keep going. I hope I will always make the choice to keep going, to be open, to listen, to have faith, to keep practicing, to love, and to be loved.

I hope you will too.

Some Final Thoughts on Grief and Loss

While my intention has always been only to share my story about how Grief showed up and inspired me to make some changes in my life, I acknowledge that some people who read this book will be seeking advice on how to deal with grief. I am often asked how I made it through my grief. This is that story. In compiling this story, I have come to understand grief as something more permanent than many of us imagine. Rather than being a state one is in temporarily, I think of it as an emotion that we experience often and always as we navigate all the losses we are subjected to in our lives.

To anyone seeking advice on navigating grief: forget everything you think you know about grief. Allow yourself to experience it through the eyes of a small child. At two or three, you don't yet have a voice of judgment persuading you to do anything other than be present in the moment. You have no expectations. If someone walks by and grabs your teddy bear right out of your arms, you are indignant. You react uncensored. You are unapologetic.

Whatever comes up for you—anger, sadness, desperation, rage, worry, fear, anxiety, or relief—allow yourself to feel every single one of those feelings. Sit still with those feelings. Listen to what they have to tell you.

It may sound strange to suggest that you wouldn't allow yourself to feel your feelings, but American society doesn't support feelings in all shapes and lengths and sizes. We prefer short-lived discomfort. We put limits on our sadness. We are asked to control our anger. We profit from selling products and pharmaceuticals that make us happy and keep us happy. We are asked to "get over it," to "move on," and to cherish our memories. That's it. Very simple instructions for an otherwise complicated undertaking (life).

When my dad died, I had to relearn how to feel my feelings. I am still learning. Anger is a tough one for me. I struggle to express anger in healthy ways. I'm working on it though. Feeling is essential in grief. Ignoring your feelings will not make them go away. They stay with you and make themselves comfortable in your body. They may manifest when triggered again by grief or show up as as anxiety, depression, or illness. They will demand your attention in any way they can get it. They will put up a fight.

Decide how to deal with your feelings. Maybe you need to do nothing. Maybe feeling a strong emotion—screaming, crying, or shaking it out—is therapeutic, and there is nothing left to do. If the feeling lingers, you may need help letting it go. Will you have a conversation? Will you go for a run? Do a breathing exercise? Have a dance party? The trick is to feel the emotion without holding on to it. Eventually, you have to let it go. Perhaps you'll keep its message or its wisdom tucked away in your heart. That's fine. But when you're ready, release it.

Above all else, be gentle with yourself. Treat yourself like an infant. Swaddle yourself in warm blankets, fill your stomach with warm drinks, eat when you are hungry, sleep when you are tired, and do whatever it takes to claim your space and meet your needs. Cry if you have to. Then, soothe yourself with the kindest, gentlest actions and words.

You will probably need to take a stand for yourself. You are likely to run into someone who wants you to walk with Grief speedily and with less sadness in your eyes. It is imperative that you also reject the judgment and expectations other people have about your grief and grieving. Nobody wants to see you hurting, but some people are better equipped than others to sit alongside you when you are hurting. Find someone who can sit with you—with no expectations about how you grieve or how long it takes. Find someone who will not judge your unique relationship with Grief. Tune the others out. Their reactions to your grief are only reflections of their own relationships with loss; another person's reaction to your grief has nothing to do with you.

In summary, with the utmost care—and while rejecting all forms of judgment and expectations—allow your feelings to rise. Feel them, listen to them, and learn from them. Feelings are merely messengers. Release what no longer serves you and repeat the process.

For better or for worse, this is an ongoing process. We will grieve many things and often at the same time. We can't predict how long it will take. Grief doesn't follow a timeline. It doesn't take a linear path. A lot of conflicting emotions can happen at once. It is confusing sometimes. Most of the time. All the time?

Make peace with the possibility that whatever you experience—no matter how outlandish or inappropriate or dubious it may seem—is completely normal. Your grief is unique. It will not look like your best friend's grief or your sister's grief. It may not even look the same as it did last time. It is unpredictable. Grief may be a constant in our lives, but the feelings we feel are not permanent; they will pass. Let Grief have its way with you.

If the thought of being broken open by loss scares you, and you're struggling to see your way through grief, think of yourself as an old home that needs renovating. You might have great bones, but you could use some updates. The demolition is likely to be painful. It is in and of itself destructive, but once it is finished and all the rubbish is cleared away, there are more open spaces. In those spaces, you will rebuild. You will be refurbished with better-functioning parts. You will become more energy efficient. More light will come in through your windows. You will sparkle. Down the road, you might need some additional repairs. You may outgrow your space and need to build an addition. You may always be under construction in some way. At the same time, no matter what needs attention, you will be fully functioning. It may require making some special accommodations, but you are always livable. There isn't anything wrong with needing to grieve a loss. It's something we get to do as humans—as homes to our beautiful spirits.

While I anticipate that struggle almost always accompanies loss, I know from personal experience and from what I have heard from others, that the strength of loss is in its power to transform. It can transform you. Every step of the way, you get to choose what do next. Perhaps I harbor some fear that I will have to make another choice about where to go from wherever I am when loss hits the next time; however, I know that I am not at the mercy of my losses.

I hope I will always choose to remain in my power. As much as I allow my grief to have its way with me, in the end, I hope I will have my way with it. And I hope the same for you.

Writing Exercise: Neverness

In the writing class I took with my mom and sister, our instructor Kathryn Holl assigned us to write about "Neverness" (what would never be as a result of the loss we were experiencing). I highly recommend this absolutely heart-wrenching exercise. I found it incredibly cathartic to acknowledge what will never be.

In the process of calling the neverness out of the darkness and into the light, my fears about having to face my life without my dad lost some of their power over me. To give you an example of what this writing exercise might look like, I share an unedited version of the assignment here.

> I will never again know the feeling of my dad's beard scratching my face as he hugs me good-bye. I will never get to say good-bye. I will never get another hug from my dad. I will never reach for my dad's freckled hand to give it a squeeze, noting how it has aged since my last touch, appreciating its strength, and remembering how it used

to gently brush my hair and pull it back into a ponytail when I was a little girl. We had matching ponytails for a while, and when he died, he again had a very long ponytail. When he started growing his hair out, President Bush was in office (W). None of us were huge fans of his plan to grow out his hair so he said he would cut his hair again when a Democrat took office. But he didn't cut it. He will never cut that ponytail.

I will never hear my dad say, "Anna Bandana!" or "Anna Bear!" when I call. He always acted so happy to hear from me, even if he had just left my house. He will never come to my house. He will never babysit my children in a pinch. He will never bounce any of my children on his knee, reciting, "Trot, trot to Boston, trot trot to Maine, trot trot to Boston and back home again!" He will never hold them close to read them a story. He will never sing them "Near Nee Now." He will never hear my daughter, who was barely two years old when he died, sing little songs to herself as she twirls around in circles, just like I did when I was little. He will never say, "Alexander T. Cornpone!" when he sees my son Alexander. My dad will never pull up in his pickup truck to take my son James to his guitar lesson as he did every Thursday for two years before he died. He will never complain to James about the other drivers on the road all the way to and from the guitar lesson. They will never say in unison, "Dan Callan!" when they pass one of his many "Land For Sale" signs posted along the road. They will never stop for candy bars at the hardware store. They will never jam with James's guitar teacher, Tim, or make the recording they had planned to make. My dad will never attend any of my children's games or their school programs. He won't see them graduate from high school or college. He won't dance at their weddings. He will never take another vacation with us. My children will never make another memory with their Papaw. My daughter might not remember him at all.

I will never see my dad perform either alone or with his band. I'll never hear him say, "Now it's time to pause for a good cause" when it's time for a bathroom break. He will never play "Amazing Grace" before Thanksgiving dinner. I will never stand there, worrying that the food is getting cold, trying to appreciate the beauty of the moment as all the people I love the most stand around one table together, listening to

my dad sing one of the most moving songs
on earth. He will never eat the dark meat.
He will never take leftovers home to enjoy
later. He will never nod off on the sofa, then
wake up irritated, ready to go. He will never
grow impatient with my mom as he waits
for her to get out the door.

He will never bring tea to my mom in
the morning or rub her feet at night. They
will never watch another obscure movie
together, then tell me about it afterward.
Separately. He will never finish all the
projects he started around the house or
in his art class. We'll never know what he
planned to do with all the sheet metal he had
gathered for his most recent sculpture. He
will never tell me about his next project. He
will never do another project. He will never
clean out his shed or put his clothes away.
He will never show up wearing a funny hat
or a cool hat. He will never buy another
T-shirt. He will never wear another T-shirt.
He will never bring me a new book to read.
He will never take one of my books home to
read. He will never sit on the toilet reading
The New Yorker. He will never sit on the
toilet. He will never sit anywhere.

My dad will never exchange a knowing
glance with my husband in the midst of the

craziness that often swirls around my mom, my sister, and me. He will never tell me how proud he is of my husband or how proud he is of me. He will never look at me and say, "You're so beautiful" as he did for as long as I can remember. He will never stare at my mom, when she isn't looking, and tell me how beautiful she is or how much he loves her. He will never share another Jamesism, like he so loved to do. "Oh! I forgot to tell you. You'll never guess what James said this time …" I'll never hear him say, "Far out." I'll never hear him laugh. I will never look over and see him wiping his eyes when he is moved to tears, which was often. He will never be there to rescue me when I need him. I will never again hear cheers or encouragement from my biggest fan. He will never defend me. I will never listen as he shares his wisdom or his unique outlook on life. He will never tell me about a story he just heard on NPR. I will never roll my eyes at one of his jokes. We will never talk politics, religion, or anything else that you aren't supposed to talk about. We will never talk again in the way I've talked to him my whole life.

This feels like maybe it could go on forever. It's breaking my heart! I will never

see my dad in his body or feel his touch
again. I don't think it matters how old a
person is when he dies, or how sick he was,
or how whatever the case may be. For the
record, my dad was young at sixty-two when
he died, and he was healthy. But no matter
what circumstances surround a loved one's
death, the absence of their physical presence
creates a hole in our lives and in our hearts. I
will never stop missing my dad's presence.
I will never stop wishing for just one more
hug. That hole will never go away.

What I know now is that even in the
absence of my dad's body, he is with me. He
is with my children. He is with my husband.
He is with my mom. He is with my sister and
with her family. He is with his friends. He is
with all the guys from all of his bands, his
buddies from work, and the people he knew
from the art classes he was taking when he
died. He is with his friend, the welding
instructor, who was deeply saddened when
he heard the news of my dad's death. He
is with Tim and James at each and every
guitar lesson. He is with his lifelong friend,
Ernest, who flew in from California to
attend his funeral. My dad was there when
some of the guys he has loved the most, guys
from his band, played "Amazing Grace" at

his funeral. And he was probably wiping tears from his eyes, moved by their loving tribute to the man he was and the influence he had on their lives. What I know now is that my dad's love continues to surround us. His spirit lives on in and around all of the people he loved. Some of the things I thought I'd never share with my dad when he died can still be shared. What I didn't know then, on the night of his death or on the day of this class, is that even though he is gone, I will never truly lose my dad.

Acknowledgments

This could be an entire book in and of itself. I often wonder what would have come of me had my fifth and sixth grade teacher, Mr. Gary Horning, not been so committed to nurturing creativity in the classroom. I have heard many stories since deciding to follow a creative path that involve a teacher or some other adult squashing a child's creative dreams. I was always lucky to have my creativity encouraged, and Mr. Horning was one of the first people, outside of my parents, who really made me believe I was capable of creating great things. Thank you, Mr. Horning. I am forever thankful for all the lessons you taught those of us who were lucky enough to be your students and for the choices you made about how we would spend our precious time together.

I've been fortunate to have a number of inspiring teachers in my life. Two professors who left the biggest impressions on me while I was a student at Michigan State University were Anita Skeen and Martin Benjamin. I consider myself very lucky to have been your student, and I will always be grateful for the ways in which you challenged me to think outside the realm of what I knew to be true in the world. There was always so much more than I had imagined.

I am grateful for my very first life coach, Ken Diller. You said, "No, Anna. What is your dream?" I will never forget your kindness or the many ways in which you encouraged me to "fly my freak flag" and share my work with the world. I'm not sure anyone would be holding this book in their hands had you not encouraged me to pursue my dream of writing it.

When I wasn't sure where to go for the kind of gentle guidance a priest might offer after my dad's death, I turned to a wise and gifted yoga teacher: Lee Ann Louis-Prescott. Lee Ann, thank you for being you and for always, and in all ways, striving to live your yoga. I am grateful.

For his passion for empowering people to tell their stories, I am so grateful to Robert Palmer of Raven Writing Studios, Ink. Thank you Robert. Your enthusiasm is contagious. I am also grateful to Marilyn Bousquin of Writing Women's Lives. Marilyn, your passion for helping women to find and use their voices is inspiring and very much appreciated. Thank you. And for the beautiful work she does in the world, helping people heal through writing, I am grateful to Kathryn Holl.

Also, for their generous teachings, faith in story, and the wealth of ways in which they inspire creativity, I am grateful to Melody Ross, Christine Mason Miller, and Pixie Lighthorse. Our paths crossed when I needed it most. Thank you.

I am ever so grateful for the insight and feedback of my dear friends and family who helped me immensely by reading early drafts of this story, specifically Kathleen, Sarah, Nikki, Michelle, Tiffany, Libby, and Heather. Your support and encouragement means the world to me. I could not have done this without you.

For sharing her beautiful photographic gifts with me, and for her friendship, I am grateful for Heather Heffley of Heather Heffley Photography. Heather, you are a light in this world.

My dear friend, Janelle DeWolf of Studio 116, captured the photo on the back cover of this book, and for that I am grateful. Thank you for sharing your gifts with the rest of us, Janelle.

It is with the help of many lovely souls who have filled the gaps on the home front over the years that I was able to write this book. Thank you, Nathan, Emily, Shannon, Pam, Tara, Madi, Larissa, and Diane. I am thankful for the many beautiful ways you have touched—and continue to touch—our lives.

I am grateful to my mom, dad, and Sarah for being my first home and for doing everything you did to cultivate and maintain that home for me. Mom and Sarah especially, thank you. No matter what we face, love prevails, and I will appreciate that for the rest of this life and for all my lives after.

I am blessed and lucky in tribe. Thank you to all our family and my dear friends who supported me after the death of my father. I would be lost without my goddesses and the many friends who carried me when I couldn't carry myself. I am grateful for the care and encouragement of my kindreds—my fellow makers. I am also extremely grateful for the lovely women who have become heart connected with me. Thank you family, friends, and sisters. You are all top-notch.

To James, Alexander, and Sophia, thank you. You may never know how much I love you or how much your support means to me. Thank you for giving me perspective and for showing me all the best ways to do life. You are, by far, my greatest teachers. I am so grateful for you and to you. I love you infinity.

And to you Daniel, you make all the dreams possible. Thank you for believing in me, supporting me, and helping me in every way and on every step along the way. Thank you for listening. Thank you for seeing me and for allowing yourself to be seen by me. I am eternally grateful that we chose each other. It is a privilege to do life with you. I love you like crazy.

I would like to extend a huge thanks to Balboa Press and especially to my editor, Chris. I am grateful for those who embrace the mystery—the mystics, healers, storytellers, teachers, guides, and medicine people of our time. And finally, thank you to the universe for whispering in my ear, inviting me to share my story, and rising up to meet me all along the way.

With a full heart, I thank you. I am complete.

Bibliography

Elisabeth Kübler-Ross and David Kessler, *On Grief and Grieving: Finding the Meaning of Grief through the Five Stages of Loss* (New York: Scribner, 2005).

Michael Rosen and Helen Oxenbury, *We're Going on a Bear Hunt* (New York: Aladdin Books, 1992).

About the Author

Photo by Heather Heffley

Anna Hodges Oginsky holds a bachelor's degree in humanities from Michigan State University and a master's degree in social work from the University of Michigan. Her work is inspired by spirituality, creativity, and cultivating community.

Anna lives in Brighton, Michigan, with her husband and their three children.

Printed in the United States
By Bookmasters